Like A Boss

Leona Burton

Print ISBN: 9798392321179

1st Edition

Some names and identifying details have been changed to protect the privacy of individuals

Contents

Foreword

Oh, Rebels, do I have something to tell you!

Get ready for a book that's gonna teach you how to boss it up like a pro. That's right, we're talking about "Like a Boss", the ultimate guide to ruling the workplace.

This book is the real deal, folks. It's got all the secrets you need to know to become the boss you were born to be. And let me tell you, it's not just about barking orders and strutting around in high heels. No, no, no. "Like a Boss" is all about owning your power, being confident in your decisions, and inspiring your team to be their best selves.

The authors of this book are total Rebels, let me tell you. They know what it takes to succeed in today's world and they're not afraid to dish out the tough love. But don't worry, they're also super relatable and hilarious. You'll feel like you're chatting with your bestie over cocktails instead of reading a boring old leadership book.

And let's talk about the content. This book covers everything from how to communicate like a pro, to managing difficult personalities, to mastering your emotional intelligence. It's like having your own personal mentor, but without the high price tag.

So, if you're ready to slay your career goals and be the boss of your dreams, "Like a Boss" is the book for you. Trust me, you won't regret it. Now, go out there and kick some butt.

Much Love as always,

Leona xox

Chapter One

How To Be A Winner In Life And Business

Beth Thompson

I f you're reading this right now, then I'm going to take a bet that you're a business owner who wants to create more impact and good in the world, right? And I'll also guess you've got a pretty good vision in your head for what you want for yourown life, one which doesn't revolve around the 9-5 rat race and allows you freedom, great money and the luxury of choice. Time to spend with your family. An income that satisfies your drive.You're probably someone who has a fire in their belly and ambition in their heart to take up space, do more good and leave this world a little bit better than it is right now. And yet...Even with all that want and determination and talent, there's something that's holding you back from showing up as your fully fucking wonderful self? Something that's stopping you from showing up as you? Guess what? I know because I've been there.

I've always wanted to own my own business, even from way back when I was a little girl. I eventually went to university at Leeds Metropolitan (as it was known back then) to study Public Relations and Communications, with a dream of one day opening my own PR agency. But it didn't play out like I thought it was going to happen. My own career got a bit sidetracked along the way- by this I mean I met my wonderful husband James when I was still at university and found out I was pregnant while still studying. I eventually graduated at 36 weeks pregnant with a 2.1 and had my first son Logan 2 weeks later. You can imagine my surprise when I then had my second son Rory, just 13 months later.Being 'mummy' to 2 children under 2, 24 hours a day meant the idea of going off and working for somebody else just wasn't going to happen.

It's a fact that childcare in this country costs an absolute fortune, and after eventually reducing our household income and going down to one wage, by late 2018 we found ourselves in the midst of £35k worth of debt. If you've ever been in debt, you'll probably understand better than anyone when I say I felt like I had a black mark against my name. I didn't tell anyone about the situation- I was embarrassed and ashamed, and to be really honest, I felt pretty worthless. I remember sitting at the kitchen table in the hazy heat of the August of that year, watching my two chunky toddlers pottering about and thinking to myself 'I've GOT to do something'. In that moment, I decided to stop feeling sorry for myself, looked at what I could do, what I was actually good at, and decided to do something about it.

Writing.

Communicating.

Brand building.

Selling.

Persuasion.

I knew I was bloody good at writing, I loved it. I didn't care at that point who I would end up writing for- I just wanted to do something myself to help us get out of the shit that we'd found ourselves in. The first time I ever got paid, I cried. It was for writing two articles about buy-to-let properties and mortgages (which was about as appealing to me as watching paint dry). The sheer relief of feeling like my idea had legs, that I could charge for my talents and contribute to getting us out of the red, made my eyes leak happy tears. I vowed in that moment to do everything in my power to help us stabilise financially. That first freelance job paved the way for me to see what was possible; I could finally see a way to make my dream of starting my own business a real, viable thing. And if I could get paid for doing work I really didn't care about, then imagine the kind of impact I could create when it was for clients that really lit me up?

A couple of years later, DARE Copywriting was born. That initial dream of owning my own business turned into a full blown sales copywriting agency, helping ambitious brands to show up, stand out and sell more with their words. I've worked with clients and companies from all over the globe, helping them to elevate their messaging, perfect their positioning, and attract more clients with unignorable copy and content. But even though I was out there, making moves, trying my hardest and my revenue was good, I was still holding myself back. The debt was still there. I was working 6am until 6pm, six days a week, constantly focused on making that next sale to try and offset the mess I felt I'd created. I was also riddled with Imposter Syndrome. One of my biggest values is authenticity, yet I felt like I was lying to not only everyone else, but myself. I was walking around, coaching my clients to 'speak from the heart' and 'show up as themselves' in their messaging and copy, yet I wasn't doing it myself. Something much deeper was going on. I couldn't physically bring myself to acknowledge how bad things had gotten. I wasn't investing in my business because quite honestly, I didn't have a pot in which to proverbially piss in. Everything I generated revenue-wise went back out at the end of the month, my credit score was in the toilet, and I was carrying a secret that made me feel like shit 99% of the time.

In early 2021, I was scrolling through Facebook when I saw a call-out for contestants on a new ITV game show. The top prize was £250,000. £250k. I sat and looked at the ad, imagining what that would be like to have as mine. To wake up and feel the weight of that debt gone, in one easy move. I could write it all off, start again. Come out from hiding and start doing the things I wanted to do. Give my children everything I wanted for them and more. And I'd be free from the shackling feeling of shame. The thought of it all was too much.

I wanted it too much. I dismissed it, closed the app, and told myself 'things like that don't happen to people like me'.

I'm going to introduce you to a concept now that literally changed the trajectory of my life. I was sat watching Netflix with my husband and the boys, a couple of days after seeing the advert for the gameshow on ITV. We were watching a film called 'We Bought A Zoo' and there's a quote in the middle of that film that spoke to me on a level I can't quite explain to you right now in words. "You know, sometimes all you need is twenty seconds of insane courage. Just literally twenty seconds of embarrassing bravery. And I promise you, something great will come of it." That realisation literally stopped me in my tracks. It all became really clear at that moment what I needed to do. It changed my thinking and would completely pivot the way I approached my business. Because I started asking myself some really big questions. Why am I limiting myself? Why shouldn't things happen for me? Why not me? Who the heck am I making myself quiet for? Why am I hiding? What was the difference between me and anyone else I'd seen absolutely killing it with their business online, trailblazing through the entrepreneurial space, or taking up space on tv? There wasn't one. There was no fundamental difference between me and them.

For the first time in my life, I realised that all the thoughts and stories I'd told myself in my head since I had been a girl, things like I was 'too loud' or 'too much' or 'not good enough'...they were all crap. It wasn't that these people were 'better' than me or that they had something that I didn't. The only thing that was at all different was the fact they'd put themselves out there and put their blumming hand up to give things a go. They'd taken the opportunity when it presented itself, snatched that right up, and done something about it. They'd put themselves into the spotlight, without a second glance back at the opinions of anyone else. They were carving out their own path. They'd made moves. So I decided to do the same. I did it. I opened the app back up, found the ad, and applied to be on Moneyball. I got through all three interview phases for that gameshow and was offered a filming slot. And guess what? On the 29th September 2021, I won £61,000. On a tv set in Media City, stood next to Ian Wright. I wrote all of my debt off in one go. That heavy, draining feeling, that weight I was carrying around? It was lifted off me in one go. For the first time in six years, I felt like I could breathe.That whole experience taught me some fundamental lessons that I'm going to share with you in this chapter.

1. Opportunity isn't reserved for anyone.

I'm starting with this one because it's probably the heftiest. There are no limitations on who gets to go for it in life. We all start from different places, different privileges, and unfortunately success is sometimes easier for those who do have that extra leg up from the get go. But I honestly believe that opportunity is EVERYWHERE. Opportunity can be created. And it's up to us as entrepreneurs to get creative, to be relentless, seek I out and take it wherever we can. I said right at the start of this chapter that I'm guessing you have a vision for what you want to do and where you want to go with your life and your business. I know this because each and every person who sets out to become a business owner has a dream in their heart to generate fantastic money for themselves, doing something they genuinely believe is needed in the world.

Don't let that vision disintegrate in the weeds of the day to day. Keep it firm in your head. Write that bugger down. Get it somewhere you can see it every single day. And if the opportunity arises to take one step closer towards that vision, whether it be telling your audience every single day exactly what you do and how you can change a person's life, or it's raising your hand to guest star on a podcast and increase your visibility, stretch out your arms and scoop them up wherever you can. You have nothing to lose and potentially everything to gain.

2. Why NOT me?

We all have a shitty committee that lives in our own head- the negative voices and mind monkeys that rear their ugly faces to whisper their totally unhelpful (and often totally false) opinions. In my case, they used to hold several meetings a day and it was more of a bellow than a quiet whisper. You see, I'm a person with a fairly big personality... Who'd have guessed that, huh? My dad was in the army and so I moved around every two years or so from one posting to the next. I was perpetually the new kid until I went to boarding school later in my early teens. Children naturally are inquisitive and so every time I would rock up to a new school, sometimes in a completely new country, I felt constantly ridiculed and under a large spotlight that I never asked to be under. I was told I was 'too loud' 'Too intimidating'

'Too weird' 'Too much' It took me until I was 30 years old to realise that I was still carrying these opinions around in my own head and it was affecting me as an adult. Filtering myself for people who no longer were even in my life. I was still trying to please people whose opinions had literally no bearing on my life now.

Here's the tea: you will never be 'too much' or 'too anything' for the right people. It might sound counterintuitive but the more you let your guard down, the more you let people see you for who you truly are, the easier it is to attract the right people into your life, whether that's in your personal relationships or your professional life. You can't please everyone. You never will. You can't make everyone like you. If you set out to try and do that, you're setting yourself up for failure from the get go.Your authenticities, your quirks, your personality, the way you operate; that's the stuff that makes you YOU and it's the stuff that separates you from everyone else in your industry that's doing the same thing. If you're building a brand, play to those strengths. Yeah, you'll turn some people off. But you'll also be like catnip to the people who think you're the cat's pyjamas. That's how you keep people in your world. You're freaking fantastic just as you are. The whole world deserves to see you in all your authentic glory. So let them see you.

3. Forget about the outcomes

I know I've just spent a whole paragraph or two telling you why you should focus on your vision and what you want, and so maybe you're now reading this thinking' what?!' Just stick with me, ok? It's so, SO easy to get consumed by the doing when you're working towards a goal, and I don't think this is probably more true than when you're preparing to launch a new offer or product. We've all done it. We've mapped out the campaign, worked out the strategy, looked at the numbers and put our best foot forward when preparing to launch. You want the best results possible; the right amount of sales, achieving x amount of audience growth. And when you're in the middle of all that showing up, serving your audience and hoping it goes to plan, it can be so easy to lose faith and start questioning things in the middle of all that energy.

In my humble opinion, the more you forget about the outcome and trust the process, the better you'll always do. Winners don't focus on their competition or start changing things on race day; they focus on their own game. They stay in their own lane. They look forward, not backwards or to the side at what anyone else is doing. Trusting yourself and trusting the process is a big lesson to learn but it's been one of the most crucial learnings I've taken away in the time my business has been operating. You know your stuff. You're a ridiculously capable and talented human. Lean into the process and don't sweat the small stuff.

4. Get Your Ass in The Arena

Shortly after I won the money, I was browsing through Netflix again (I know, it's kind of my self-care happy place to flick through and find a murder doc or some kind of gritty drama). On this occasion, I came across a documentary called The Call To Courage by TEDx speaker, author, podcast host, and researcher, Brené Brown. I'd had some press about the big win, and of course, checked out Twitter to see how it was being received. It wasn't great. Well, that's putting it mildly. I think Twitter can be a murky place. The trolls were rife, and in my head I knew rationally it was probably jealousy that was fuelling the comments but in my heart, it hurt. All of those old feelings of being called out, feeling exposed, and vulnerable flooded to the surface.

Instead of celebrating, I felt like retreating, and Netflix seemed a good place to hide. In my ignorance, I didn't really know who Brené Brown was or a lot about her work but I had heard really good things through friends and connections in the online space, and so decided to give her documentary a bash. It always sounds dead corny to say but the 1 hr and 16 minutes that I watched Brené Brown speaking to her audience about vulnerability, shame and courage turned my understanding of myself and my own purpose on its axis. It was like everything I believed about standing out, showing up proudly, despite the feeling of wanting to hide, was suddenly amplified. Brené Brown is someone who's spent her whole life researching shame, leadership and human behaviour.

There's a specific section in the documentary where she's talking about receiving negative criticism after putting herself out there on stage. She was mortified reading the comments section and wanted to hide from all the negativity. When doom- scrolling on the internet, she came across a quote from Theodore Roosevelt that fundamentally impacted her life: "It is not the critic who counts: not the man who points out how the strong man stumbles or where the doer of deeds could have done better. The credit belongs to the man who is actually in the arena, whose face is marred by dust and sweat and blood, who strives valiantly, who errs and comes up short again and again, because there is no effort without error or shortcoming, but who knows the great enthusiasms, the great devotions, who spends himself in a worthy cause; who, at the best, knows, in the end, the triumph of high achievement, and who, at the worst, if he fails, at least he fails while daring greatly, so that his place shall never be with those cold and timid souls who knew neither victory nor defeat." It changed her whole life and what she had to say about her experience changed mine: "There's millions of cheap seats in the arena that are filled with people who never venture onto the floor. They never put themselves out there. They just hurl mean-spirited criticisms and put downs from a safe distance.

Therefore, we need to be selective about the feedback we let into our lives. Don't hold those opinions close from people who aren't being brave with their lives, who aren't showing up. If you're not in the area getting your ass kicked, I'm NOT interested in your feedback." In that moment I realised that I wasn't alone. In fact. I'd probably never felt more seen. Because like Brené, I want to create things. I want to help people. I want to be brave with my life. I love what I do, I love my work, and I'll continue to challenge myself, to be uncomfortable because that's where growth happens. It became really clear that I had a choice. I could decide to stop taking on criticisms from people who literally would never have the guts to do what I did. To stop listening to anyone who wasn't being brave with their life, whose values didn't really align with my own. You have that same choice. It's not about not caring what other people think; it's about understanding that if the person who's criticising you doesn't align with the values that you have for your own life, you have zero obligation to take their opinion as fact. They're not in the arena, fighting the same fight as you. I want to be in that arena.

Are you coming with me?

I called this chapter 'If not you, who? If not now, when?' because I want you to really think about that question and how you want to answer it. I'm going to tell you what I know to be the answer:

It is you.

It is now.

Seize those opportunities, show up, put yourself out there authentically, get your ass in the arena, and be brave with your life.

You've got this. And I believe in you.

Chapter Two

How Body Confidence Impacts Your Results In Business

Miranda Christopher

It's reported that over 90% of women suffer with body confidence issues at some stage of their lives. As someone who experienced a very public humiliation on my physical shape at the age of 10, I can truly relate to this statistic. As a result of my experience, I yo-yo dieted for most of my teenage and adult life. Spending so much time and energy on the hamster wheel of losing and gaining weight. Never ever happy with myself, berating myself constantly with that noisy critic in my head. "Who do you think you are", "what the hell do you think you look like". Always comparing myself to others. Not really understanding why I felt this way. Someone once shared with me that "how we do one thing in life is how we do everything", I've got to say that I really didn't get that until I did my research into female entrepreneurship after the collapse of my own highly successful and very lucrative transformation consultant business in 2014.

I experienced burn-out with a life changing illness.

My body said enough was enough. And therein began my pity party for one. The illness resulted in me being unable to speak without slurring, unable to retain my balance, living with the most excruciating pain in my head; and having a mind full of jumbled thoughts that just spued out like a fountain of total nonsense. It really put the focus on all the things that weren't working for me in life, me. After four months of living like a hermit, shopping only online and eating nothing but white food - because something had reset in my brain to think that all food consumed should be clean - with the help of my husband I finally ventured outside. I remember getting the dis-approving looks because I was slurring and stumbling, clinging to my husband's arm. It was like that public humiliation as a child all over again.

I felt shame with my illness. In the year that passed before I ventured out on my own, I had piled on weight. Well, with nothing to do, nowhere to go and lots of white bread to eat, it's not such a surprise. I was hiding behind my body's additional coat of fat. My own body confidence was at an all time low. As a result of not being able to do the organisational transformation work, I loved so much, I sought out other passions I could pursue. As a child I would love to create clothing for the paper dolls you cut out from girls' magazines. And my dog, Bobby, provided me with ample opportunity to dress him and take him on his very own 'Dog Walk' in my little sister's pram. Up and down the street we strutted, without a care in the world. That was, until my mum found out I had taken the pram again and cut up a piece of clothing she wasn't quite finished with.

One of the things I did in recovery was to train as a Style Coach®, passing with a distinction in record time. Hey, there is a blessing in every situation, right? I might not have been very outwardly mobile, but my I was ready for change. Doing the Style Coaching, a fusion of internal and external change, gave me the impetus to get out of my pity party for one and start to reconnect with people, particularly women. I attended a personal development event just for women and noticed a very interesting phenomenon. It turned out that most of the audience were female entrepreneurs. What I found fascinating, sitting there feeling like a total fraud, was that I recognised that I wasn't the only one feeling that way. The words spoken were not congruent with their body language and how they were dressed. Some of the attendees were speaking about were their successes, which were impressive. Yet the energy of words delivered was that of doubt and being a fraudster; like they weren't worthy of their achievements. There were others in the room who I could see really struggled to be in the room, it was obvious to me that it had taken a mammoth step for them to actually be there, sadly most of them remaining silent during the sessions. Once again, I could relate.

What started as a simple curiosity, actually turned into a three- and half-year research project asking the question "why do women fail in business". The project switched focus part way through, turning it into a set of findings of "what women need to succeed". It was a long journey that thankfully I was able to undertake at my own pace through my own recovery. What a journey. With much gratitude to a brilliant coach who is a highly successful author, I was able to turn my findings into a pocket guide "Minerva, A Manifesto for Women Who Want to Do Business, Make Money and Enjoy Life" (available on Amazon).

Whilst this Minerva project was ongoing, I had decided to, in a very small way, offer my Style Coaching services focused on body confidence. It was a privilege and honour to work with the women who came to me, yet it was also overwhelming and left me drained and in bed for days after I had worked with them. I found myself sat in front of beautiful everyday women, just like you and me, who had experienced some form of trauma in life and were struggling with how they looked and what they wore. OMG. What do they say, "When the student is ready, the teacher shows up"! I realised that in sharing their stories with me, they were taking me on my own journey of recovery beyond the physical ailments. I came to understand from my own experiences that we perpetuate situations and experiences in life by being totally embedded in our own stories. Like the "this is the way it is round here" that I used to hear in corporate transformations.

Learning Point: Being aware of our back story is the first step into transforming into the person we want to be, who we truly are - before life left it's imprint of who we believed we should be.

In my research, I was able to see how our stories were played out time and time again and I came to understand that we each have a hidden rulebook of how our life should be. I continued my learning journey beyond the Minerva project. Whilst conducting my interviews with hundreds and hundreds of women, I started to notice that there were a handful of women who were different from the rest. They projected an air of quiet confidence, spoke in a calm way, and shared how balance in all things was a key for their success. Quite frankly, they mystified me, I knew they had sussed something that most people never do. Everything seemed so easy and effortless for them. And, as that has not been my experience of life thus far, I wanted to know more about how they achieved their successes.

I studied teachings of the ancients, of the Alchemists moving right through to modern day biochemistry and neuroscience. I massively invested in myself with leading teachers at a time when financial reserves were low. As I progressed on my journey with the old teachings explained in a new way through modern science, I noticed how the money came in when it felt like the next step was the right step for me. What I came to understand was that, from being in the womb to the age of around four years, our unique rulebook is formed based on the environment we find ourselves in. This rulebook has as its foundations our core beliefs formed through a survival instinct, not wanting to be eaten by the sabre tooth tiger. Bizarre right, we are still shaping our lives from a fear of being eaten by a cat that has been extinct for millions of years. Those core beliefs, or "wounds", are how we see ourselves as individuals separate from our mother and father figures and the world around us. The two biggest ones being the mother wound of "not worthy enough" and the father wound of "not good enough". Both, I wore like a suit of armour against the world. And trust me these wounds show up in the oddest of ways, as they filter our experience of life and what we believe is the truth about ourselves.

As we grow, the rulebook develops from the conditioning of the world around us, by the cultures such as religion, the education system, our peers and from society as a whole. All based on the filters of our core wounds. I was born with parents who were emotionally unavailable, that's why my rulebook has very strong not worthy and not good enough vibe to it. I experienced violence, physical and emotional harm from being inside the womb. For me the world was most definitely an unsafe place. Life was a battlefield. I was told that "little girls should be seen and not heard". I had to dress a certain way, and I was always getting into trouble for doing things that kids naturally do, like getting covered in mud when they are having mud fights with neighbouring children.

Rules. Rules. Rules. When my parents split, it was interesting to see the reactions of our fellow Catholic church goers. My dad had never been big into religion and rarely attended church. He only converted to Catholicism to marry my mum. Spot the rule? You must join our club to have what you want. Pile on top of that all the teachings that I was exposed to daily; women are not worthy; you are not good enough because you are not a man. Rules on how to dress, what to say and how to behave. Rules imposed by a certain sector of society that didn't have the interests of all in mind. So many women lose the sense of who they are and place themselves at the bottom of the pile of needs, all because of made up rules. And let's not forget the office filling sausage machine that our education establishment is today. No longer are children allowed to play and explore who they are and what their passions might be. All in favour of bums on seats, a rigid "one size fits all" curriculum that leads to the one route of the steadfast target of "good grades". Can you feel me seething at this point? With neurodivergent kids and grandkids, trust me, I've experienced the rigidity first hand.

My career took me into the space of large organisations, particularly financial and the government organisations. Well hello to the boy's club. Some of you may struggle with what I am going to say now; I am not a supporter of equality in the workplace. These organisations and their hierarchical structures were created by a few elitist males for their own benefit, designed for men. And yes, some things have changed, but not enough. Women have been jumping through hoops to fit into a world that wasn't designed for them, for their phases and cycles of life. Equality gives you the right to operate in a world not designed for women.

Give me equity any day. A world of work that provides the right environment for each diverse group's needs. But hey, the current day organisation structures and working practices were based on the military, and if you are not in the boy's club, you are cannon fodder. And by the way, that applies to a lot of men too. Is it any wonder that so many women are choosing their own pathway after pregnancy and when experiencing the menopause?

Learning Point: Understanding why how the rulebook plays out in your life gives you the opportunity to make conscious considered decisions for your life and business.

Now, how does this relate to body confidence and getting the results you desire in business? When we make a change to our identity, for example we move from being employed to self- employed, the hidden rulebook isn't concerned about where you are going and what you are doing. It has one function, to keep the game the same – to ensure that you survive. It keeps us in our self- made limited box. Your rulebook will unconsciously generate a whole load of poop for you to deal with to distract you from where you are going. For example, if you believed like me that you had to look a certain way to be a stylist then guess what, you are not going to put yourself out there.

I had plenty of opportunities when I started my style coaching practice to speak about what I do and why expressing who we are through what we wear is important for our business. I would find that I ended up having to reschedule because I had a sore throat, or I would feel so anxious that I'd talk myself out of it. But here's the interesting thing about this, I was no stranger to public speaking or addressing global directors or politicians. I remember walking into a room of directors on behalf of one of my managers who had felt bullied by them, to be met with the response "oh f%@k, it's her". They knew they I wouldn't tolerate the way they behaved.

As I said, my body weight dramatically increased as I started to share about my new business, another way my rulebook was seeking to stop me. Perceiving myself as unattractive and "hefty" was a safety mechanism to ensure I didn't show up. No showing up meant, I limited my exposure, which meant that I didn't get clients. And then no one would find out I wasn't good enough. You see, I discovered that we exist in three states in life.

We are either:

- Stuck where we are, unable to make any kind of progress,

- Oscillating, going for what we want and then bouncing right back to where we were (or worse). Think yo-yo dieting or the famine or feast of business cashflow.

- In Flow. Moving easily and effortlessly towards what we want, taking the challenges of everyday life in our stride.

Just like the small group of women from my research project. And there are two ways of being stuck; doing nothing or doing everything so we have too much on our plates to progress. Our rulebook really is a sneaky little life limiting sucker. You'd think that being able to see the rulebook for what it was and understanding how it plays out in your life would be enough, wouldn't you? Oh no. That rulebook isn't done with you yet.

One of the findings that I came across, in my original research was that most of the women interviewed didn't have a vision for their life, which guaranteed that they didn't hold a vision for their business. And if we have no vision, how the hell do we know where we are going? Some people mistake this for "being in flow", it's not flow – water only flows when there is a differential. From one place to another, from the mountains via the rivers to the sea. You flow from your current situation to your vision. And there's the rulebook again. No vision means no flow, which means you stay the same.

So, you have a vision, everything is going to be okay, right? Not necessarily. For those who had a vision, except the small group of women, it turned out to be a negative vision. A vision focused on fixing something rather than creating something you love. Until we see and understand the rulebook, enabling us to make conscious decisions, human beings experience life in a state of resolving their wounds. I'm not good enough drove me to excel in a male dominated environment, working harder, precariously balancing family and career, achieving so much more than my male counterparts. It meant I had to have a raft of qualifications to say, yes, I am good enough. It also provided a significant contribution to my burn-out. This ongoing need to resolve our identity, to fix ourselves is what has created a multibillion-dollar personal development industry. Right alongside an equally massive media industry – also controlled by men – telling us as women what we should be, do and have. When our vision is outside the rulebook of how our life should be, we are able to make truer choices for ourselves. Choices that really do make our hearts' sing. Learning Point: True vision and choices are free of any conditioning or beliefs that come from our rulebook.

There are more possibilities than you can imagine, you just have to learn to tune into them. Studying all the leading lights and having teachers who opened the doors of possibility for me, along with a massive dose of intuitive insight, meant that I was now able to develop a framework that enabled women to be just like those women "in flow" that I had interviewed. Seeing and being who they choose to be. Getting the results in life they truly desired. This framework focuses on the supportive energy states for women moving through the cycles of life.

I asked a number of women to join me as testers whilst I developed and piloted 'Activate the Goddess Within™', my framework. One of them was a very good friend who had also experienced burn-out in her life, leading to her closing her marketing agency of eighteen years. When I had that conversation with her, you know how it goes: "What are you up to?", my friend Judith "Sat on the sofa, waiting for something to come along". Big eye roll from me. This is a classic being "stuck" scenario. Dear reader, if there's one thing, I am very certain of, you must get off your butt and take action. No action means you float around like flotsam on the big pond of life, travelling at the will of outside circumstances. Thankfully, Judith acted and felt so transformed that she jumped at the chance to join me teaching this different way of being to other women.

Those women in the research, the "in-flow" women, had one thing in common. They were all living a life they loved. Doing what they loved. Making money from what they loved. That didn't mean they floated through life on a cloud like some ethereal goddess. It meant that when life presented challenges, they had the capability to see it for what it was and choose their response.

"Between stimulus and response there is a space. In that space is our power to choose our response. In our response lies our growth and our freedom."

As I was learning from my many teachers, it struck me that I hadn't really being making conscious choices about my own life. And certainly not my business. Those passions from childhood had fallen by the wayside when it came to being streamed into subjects for end of school exams. As an 'intelligent girl' at a Catholic girl's school, I was coerced into subjects that, yes, I was good at, but had very little passion for. I wanted to carry on with needlework, with art and cooking but was told I wouldn't get a good career from those; those were the subjects for girls who were to become home makers. My passion for art, for design and clothing had slipped into the rulebook as non-options for me. My first loves had tried to surface many times but were always overshadowed by more important things. Usually other people's agendas.

In January 2022, I made the conscious choice to focus on my health and wellbeing, by no longer yo- yo dieting. In February 2022, I bought a sewing machine. Just a simple, cheap machine to explore as a hobby. That way, if it fell by the wayside again, it hadn't cost too much. What had I really lost? Can you see the "not good enough" there? May that same year, at the time of writing this only eight months ago, I started a foundation course in Fashion Design. And I have been on the craziest ride ever since.

My rulebook has been fighting me every step of the way. Every fricking step. You wouldn't believe, the thoughts of "you are too old to do this", "you'll look stupid", "you've got to look like a stick thin teenage model to do this". This inner stress inflamed my body, which led to the sore throats, that led to a very serious chest infection, that led to taking rapid weight gaining drugs (stated side effect) – preferable to not being able to breathe. All driven by the rulebook to stay safe. The irony of my situation is not lost on me. Throughout I have remained connected to my vision and true choice and kept moving forward, kept taking the next action. I "alchemised" the psychological poop that showed up; freeing the energy that it takes to hold that structure created by the rulebook, for use in creating my vision. It does take a lot of energy to maintain the rulebook.

Learning Point: When you are consistently connected to your dreams, your rulebook will do everything to stop you. Tell it "thank you for sharing", see it for what it is and just take the next step.

When I started to design my new business, I knew it had to do two things: one, it had to work for me and my lifestyle choices, I had to be doing something I loved to do, and secondly be of value for the women I serve. When I was in my thirties, I visited a colour and image consultant. I was very excited as I knew I was in a rut with what I was wearing, the corporate uniform had spilled into black leggings and tops at the weekend. I mean, we all know that we can be invisible wearing baggy black clothes, right? Another eye roll from me. Anyway, after spending a good part of the day with her, I was so disappointed when she said that brown was a core colour for me. There was no way that I'd wear brown back then. What she didn't know and to be honest at that time, I didn't know, was that the home I had grown up in had brown as a principal colour. The place where I felt unloved, unwanted and had experienced violence first hand. No-one would knowingly choose to be constantly reminded of that, would they?

This is what led me to teaching women that expressing themselves is often a journey, one where they make the choices. Choices which often change with greater awareness, like with me – I love having brown in my wardrobe these days. I've known gurus to tell people to always wear the colours of their brands. See the rule? In my new business – the brand colours were developed from an outfit that I felt represented me, in that moment. And whilst I love the colours, they kind of remind me of the chocolate lime and sherbet lemon sweets that I used to buy on a Sunday on the way home from church. It's a nice memory, but it doesn't define me.

Learning Point: Be you each and every day, be the one who consciously chooses how you show up in the world. Feel who you are from deep within you. Design your wardrobe based on you, not the environment you work in.

A client I worked with in the early days of my style coaching, believed that she had to suit and boot for sales meetings. In her previous employment she had worn very casual clothes. When we met, she was struggling to close any sales. Together we explored who she was, what she wanted to express and what she felt good about. The suits got shown the door and a much more relaxed smart casual style emerged. The result? Her business literally went through the roof.

If over 90% of women struggle with body confidence, how does it impact them?

- They won't change careers, start that business, or do work that they love.

- They stay in unfulfilling relationships or are resistant to start a new one.

- They stay stuck in limited social circles, too frightened of comments from strangers.

- They won't attend network meetings, possibly feeling ashamed of who they are or that they stand out for the wrong reasons. Or if they do, they don't speak up.

- They won't have photo shoots or make videos or do livestreams.

- They don't show up consistently to make the changes they need to make.

- They, sadly, don't create a life that they truly love.

They are too focused on fixing their bodies, even when it's physically not possible. Just like Claire (not her real name), a six-foot-two goddess. Claire was desperately unhappy at the age of 20. She felt she stood out like a sore thumb. She wouldn't wear heels even though she kept buying them; She slumped her body in an attempt to make herself smaller and wore the dullest clothes to ensure she didn't stand out. And it turned out, she hated the career pathway she was on. Once Claire had gained awareness and understanding of her rulebook, she was able to make new choices for her life. She stood her full height, she glowed from the inside – and she changed her choice of career, choosing to go for what she really wanted.

The thing is, if your lack of body confidence comes from a perception that you are too large or too skinny, then, without getting stuck in fixing stuff, you can make a choice of having amazing health and wellbeing. This is exactly what I'm doing now. Imagine having that success you want and not being able to enjoy it? My approach to body confidence is different, it's very deep structure work, changing your biochemistry, your neurology and definitely your perspective on life. So, you won't be surprised to hear that my approach to creating your unique style expression, is also quite different. Whenever I was doing my big corporate transformation work, I had a philosophy which was aligned with "give a man a fish, feed him for a day. Teach a man to fish, feed him for life". It's still my way with personal transformation. Anything else, for me, is just fixing stuff over and over. I'm very much on my journey with combing my passion for style and clothing design, I have a very clear vision for what I want to create. But now, unlike with my past businesses, I am one of those "in-flow" women.

Every day, I choose to take my next obvious action knowing that I have the tools and resources to course correct along the way. I love my life. As I bring my chapter to a close, I invite you to imagine, what would your life look like if you were able to take the focus off your confidence (body or otherwise) issues, knowing that you had a clear pathway to what you desire - handling whatever life throws at you with ease. What would your life and your business look like?

Now go and create it.

Chapter Three

Plant Your Roots and Rise up!

Ruth Whyte

"**N**ot one mention of your dead husband you should be fucking ashamed ! sick tramp".

Setting aside how grammatically wrong this is, the fact that an anonymous "Sam Scott" made up a Facebook page just to send this to me on the 2nd anniversary of my husband's death in 2021, is actually pretty sad. But I would like to thank them. Whoever you are, thank you. Thank you for - after making me feel awful - pushing me to realise that this whole experience is more than just me. Of course, I knew that the death of my husband had affected many people in many ways, but this was more than that.

There is real struggle, I feel, on how to manage and channel emotions properly so that they don't swallow us up and become toxic. Reflecting on my own experience with this and how I trudged through the swamp of big emotions, and my management of them, has made me evaluate myself and my understanding of people. I am now determined to use this growing awareness to develop something that can offer people hope.

So, who am I?

Sometimes I ask myself that exact same question. When I think back to my 18-year-old self, what would she think of the 38-year-old version of me? It doesn't seem that long ago, but they are many worlds apart. For some people, life never changes in 20 years, for others it changes, shifts, spins, morphs and then some... I am one of the latter people! I will start when adulthood began. At 29 I met Christopher. We managed to pack a lot in from 2014 to 2018 until it all changed. The universe had other plans. We got married in 2016, moved abroad, had our daughter Amulree in 2017 and our life was good.

On the 5th of October 2018, our life was turned upside down when Cancer came chapping. He went to the appointment alone, thinking it was just stress and tiredness, at worst epilepsy.

The whirlwind of appointments, surgery, treatments, moving back to Scotland, being a mummy, wife, carer; I have limited memory of this time in my life. Then came the death, the loss, the funeral, the battle of emotions coming at me from all angles from family and the outside world. I navigated through this time in my life the best way I could, to the best of my ability. I got things wrong; I didn't do things I was meant to; I did things I wasn't meant to; I am human.

As years have passed, I am now left with feelings and emotions that are alien to some. An anxiety that can take you to places you never imagined existed. Grief that can weigh you down so much it is hard to get your head off the pillow. It is now 2023, 3 and a half years after his passing. I have a good life now. I have a lovelyhome, a supportive partner, a healthy and happy little girl, and I am grateful for all of it.

There is that part of me that is still broken and in the process of lifelong healing. But through it all, I have hope. I have hope that I will feel better, I have hope that my journey will inspire people and I have hope that I can use my pain and turn it into a purpose.

My Method

To cultivate this hope, and manage my emotions, specifically anxiety, I have dug deep and found healing through hypnotherapy and spirituality. I have taken what I have learned and created 'The Portal of Hope', a strategic process of healing and empowerment, to support anxiety management, combining hypnosis and the Chakra System.

My method offers an 8-module programme which includes: 8 guided self-hypnosis scripts, a workbook and other hints and tips to support anxiety management. The first module being an introduction to self-hypnosis, leading into 7 more modules incorporating self-hypnosis with Chakra healing. The method can be used over and over again, in any order and can be dipped into whenever needed. However, for the purpose of my chapter, I will provide you with a sneak peak of the Chakras and how they work.

Hypnotherapy

Myths: "hypnotherapy can make you do weird things", "hypnotherapy can make you feel out of control", "I can get stuck in hypnosis" just to name a few. There are so many misconceptions around hypnotherapy. So, let me just explain a little about it and how it works. The hypnotic experience begins with you. Once you decide that it is time to take a step towards healing yourself, your subconscious mind starts to prepare. You will then start to notice things around you, guiding you towards the right healing and hypnosis for you. This might be in a TV advert, on Facebook, in a magazine or a friend might give you a recommendation. The healing journey is yours. It is not the responsibility of the therapist to 'fix' you. They are only there as your guide.

The goal of hypnotherapy is to access the subconscious mind and offer positive suggestions and affirmations that create emotional and behavioural change. Through guided relaxation, which is the first step to accessing the subconscious mind, the mind and body is relaxed into a trance-like state with a focus on you being fully in control. Through my method, I offer a self-hypnosis script for each module, incorporating healing for anxiety with the use of the Chakra System structure.

Next, let's talk about chakras!

In Sanskrit, the word Chakra means 'disc' or 'wheel and it refers to the energy portals located along the spine. The Chakras are perceived by many to be spinning wheels of energy that are located at the lower back, navel, middle torso, heart, throat, forehead and just above the crown of the head. These wheels of energy keep the nervous systems, organs, and energetic body in balance. Understanding how the Chakras work is key to identifying where our issues lie so we see how this manifests in our life physically, emotionally, and spiritually. We can identify this through how balanced, blocked or overstimulated the Chakra is.

When the Chakras are healthy and balanced, they are spinning at a perfect speed and are bright and vibrant. The body, brain and overall well-being is in perfect balance, life moves in harmony and every aspect is in flow. When the Chakras are blocked, they spin slowly and sluggishly, they are dull and colourless. The body can experience pain and uncomfortable sensations along with mental and physical well-being

being low. Life's path may have taken an unexpected tangent causing upset and discord.

When the Chakras are overstimulated, they can accelerate and spin rapidly, the colour is overly bright, and the body feels out of balance. The body and brain may feel sensations of anxiety, unease, uncertainty and being out of control. When there is either blockages or overstimulation in any Chakra, it can be pinpointed, and healing can be focused to that area. If something is out of balance with the body, brain or life, there is usually a Chakra that needs some attention.

Each Chakra has its individual characteristics that it identifies with, and this makes it easier to pinpoint where the healing is needed. When researching and developing The Portal of Hope, I have come up with names for each module that aligns with my mission of offering Hope, Empowerment and supporting Anxiety Management.

Here are some key points of each Chakra that may help to enhance your knowledge and lay the foundation for you for deeper healing:

1: Plant Your Roots

The first of the Chakras is called the 'Root' with its name in Sanskrit being 'Muladhara'. It is located at the base of the spine, around the perineum and is associated with the colour red and element of earth.

When researching the symbolism associated with this Chakra, I was drawn to the Lotus flower with four petals in a central square.

The healing of the Root Chakra is associated with taking life back to basics, cultivating basic needs and the survival of the physical body. Creating feelings of safety, security, and love within your own personal circle are key elements that can be enhanced when working with the Root Chakra. My method supports this healing using self-hypnosis and therapist-led deeper inner work.

When the Root Chakra is balanced there is a sense of emotional grounding, our roots feel deep, we feel that we are where we are supposed to be. There is a great satisfaction in life, and we are comfortable with the people and environment around us. We feel a great sense of love for not only ourselves but for the people and places around us. We feel emotionally balanced, and we have an abundance of self-acceptance for the reality that we are living in. We feel full of energy and in control of our lives on a physical, emotional, and spiritual level.

When our Root Chakra is healthy and balanced, we have a strong sense of belonging and being rooted and grounded to the earth in our current life. We feel love for ourselves and loved by those around us. We feel comfortable and satisfied in our own skin and an abundance of self-acceptance. In our everyday life we feel that we are in emotional balance, in control and we have lots of energy. When our Root Chakra is blocked, we can have feelings of being ungrounded, unsatisfied and anxiety can creep in. There can be physical manifestations when the

Root Chakra is blocked where we can feel unwell, drained of energy and physically weak. We can also experience issues with the lower part of the body such as: digestion issues, lower back pain and pain in the leg's feet and bones. There may also be a lack of energy and zest for life showing up in our lives. We may have escalated insecurities and feel unworthy and not good enough.

When our Root Chakra is overstimulated, it may show up in our lives as vulnerability and not being able to deal with unexpected life challenges. Hoarding may become an issue and we may feel stuck and reluctant to make any change. Here are some positive affirmations that support healing and anxiety management through the Root Chakra: I am secure and safe, and I have people around me that love me. My roots are planted deep, and I am grounded. I am happy in my body, and in control of my thoughts and feelings. I am open and ready for change, and I am in control of what I put into my body. I feel worthy and I have my place in the world.

Here are some positive affirmations that support healing and anxiety management through the Root Chakra:

- I am secure and safe, and I have people around me that love me.

- My roots are planted deep, and I am grounded. I am happy in my body, and in control of my thoughts and feelings.

- I am open and ready for change, and I am in control of what

I put into my body.

- I feel worthy and I have my place in the world.

2: Ignite Your Fire

The Second of the Chakras is called the 'Sacral' with its name in Sanskrit being 'Svadhishthana'. The Sacral Chakra is located just above the Navel area and is associated with the colour orange and element of water. When researching the symbolism associated with this Chakra, I was drawn to the Lotus flower with six petals with a central crescent representing the moon. The Sacral Chakra is associated with the joy of being alive and harnessing our inner fire. There is a strong representation of the physical pleasure of sexuality with focus on sensuality and intimacy. There is joy in being creative through this chakra and a strong sense of being spontaneous and spending time out with one's own circle. When the Sacral Chakra is balanced and healthy, life is full of wonder and happiness, we have an abundance of energy and optimism. Life seems to flow with ease, and we are open to new and pleasurable experiences. We may be creative and feel alive in our flow when we are trying new things. We are also comfortable in our own body, and we enjoy being sensual and in flow with our sexuality.

Have you ever felt that you have lost your zest for life and feel lost and numb? When this occurs, it may be that your Sacral Chakra is blocked and spinning at a low frequency. We may feel withdrawn from life, our friends, and our family. There may also be external pressures causing stagnant energy. Other manifestations of a blocked Sacral Chakra are being physically stiff, self-sabotaging with emotional eating and body dysmorphia. Overwhelm, intense anxiety and uncertainty are key indicators that the Sacral Chakra is overstimulated. We may feel that we are out of control of our thoughts and feelings which can lead to selfishness, overindulgence on food and substances and in some cases addictive behaviour.

Here are some positive affirmations that support healing and anxiety management through the Sacral Chakra:

- I enjoy and have zest for life.

- I embrace the difficult emotions and work on processing them.

- I nourish my body with plenty of water and I am in control of my addictive behaviours.

- I am at my best when my creativity flows, and I enjoy meeting new and exciting people.

- I am confident in my body, and I enjoy sex and sensual pleasure.

- I am in control of my self-sabotaging thoughts and behaviours, and I find joy in the little and big things in life.

3: Bask In Your Sunshine.

The Third of the Chakras is called the 'Solar Plexus' with its name in Sanskrit being 'Manipura'. The Solar Plexus Chakra is located at the upper stomach area and is associated with the colour yellow and element of fire. When researching the symbolism associated with this Chakra, I was drawn to the Lotus flower with ten petals with a central triangle. When reflecting on the Solar Plexus and what it is associated with, we are in flow with our personal and inner sunshine. Following our gut instinct is a key element along with psychic ability and intuition. The energy of the Solar Plexus leads us to set personal goals and tune into our ancient survival instincts. Willpower can be strong, and we can shine bright and follow our goals.

When the Solar Plexus is healthy and balanced we are focused on our achievements and accomplishments. We have an abundance of physical energy and our drive and enthusiasm to inspire others. We find that we are thinking in a flexible way and see the positives in situations. We feel that our confidence comes from within and transformations in life are imminent.

That familiar feeling of having no clear direction and feeling that people are taking us for granted is a sign that our Solar Plexus is blocked and not in a healthy flow. We can feel that life is overwhelming, heavy, and it is hard to make simple decisions. We find that we procrastinate on life decisions and hold back on things that bring joy and happiness. Panic and fear may take over and hold us back from stepping into our power, there is then a presence of a victim mentality. There is a sense of being controlled by outside influences. Overstimulation can manifest itself as: insomnia and the brain being unable to switch off. There is a constant internal struggle of competing thoughts and irritability, and nervousness can take over. Addictive personality traits can appear along with impulsiveness and lack of self-control.

Here are some positive affirmations that support healing and anxiety management through the Solar Plexus Chakra:

- I am my own sunshine. I can, and I will take back my own power.

- I am worthy of holding my boundaries and I am confident and centred.

- I am in control of my thoughts when they become overwhelming, and I am in control of my emotions and how I let people affect them.

- I am tuned in to my own intuition and I am confident in the choices I make.

- I am in control of my own life.

4: You Are the Love

The Fourth of the Chakras is called the 'Heart Chakra' with its name in Sanskrit being 'Anahata'. The Heart Chakra is in the middle of the chest and is associated with the colour green and element of air. When researching the symbolism associated with this Chakra, I was drawn to the Lotus flower with twelve petals with two triangles interlocking representing masculine and feminine.

When we think about the Heart Chakra, we can associate this with unconditional self-love. There is a key element of healing and loving oneself and to love and be loved in return. There is a strong connection to the physical world and the love we share for the planet, there is also an association that the Heart Chakra is the midpoint between the earth and heaven. When the Heart Chakra is healthy and balanced there is positive energy towards others and situations, emotions are balanced, and the heart is opened and ready to receive love. We find that care and compassion and staple characteristics and we are physically and mentally strong and flexible.

Low self-worth, self-esteem, and confidence are manifestations of a blocked Heart Chakra. We feel that our energy is stuck, and it struggles to release from the body. We can also experience feelings of being unlovable and not good enough. When this occurs, we can retreat into oneself and show no emotions. Past events can also affect the Heart Chakra energy and cause blockages. When our Heart Chakra is overstimulated, we can experience emotional exhaustion due to being highly sensitive to crowded places, situations, events, and people & responses. We can feel that our positive energy is being drained. Additionally, we can feel ourselves getting wrapped up in other people's problems and life events, feeling the need to fix it in exchange for love and attention.

Here are some positive affirmations that support healing and anxiety management through the Heart Chakra:

- I am all the love I need. I am open to love and my heart is balanced, and I am ready to receive love in abundance.

- I am in control of my heart energy when I am around crowds of people, and I am in control of who I share my love with.

- I am comfortable in my own company.

- I am in tune with both my masculine and feminine energy,

- I am worthy of love in abundance.

5: Speak Your Truth

The Fifth of the Chakras is called the 'Throat Chakra' with its name in Sanskrit being 'Vishuddha'. The Throat Chakra is located at the front of the throat to the back of the neck, and is associated with the colour light blue and element of ether. When researching the symbolism associated with this Chakra, I was drawn to the Lotus flower with sixteen petals with a circle within a triangle symbolising the creation of sound.

The most common association to the Throat Chakra is that of self-expression and speaking your truth. Being able to express emotions in a healthy way, understanding yourself, feeling comfortable speaking out and communicating with integrity are all elements associated with the Throat Chakra. Alongside this there is also self-expression through other channels such as the arts. Being able to use other ways of communication enables us to be heard on a wider scale.

When the Throat Chakra is balanced and healthy our voice is clear and confident, expression comes with ease, and we have good self-awareness enabling us to vocalise our needs clearly. Being authentic, honest, and speaking with integrity enables us to be inspirational and empowering when speaking with others through our healthy Throat Chakra. Difficulty voicing opinions and speaking your truth are feelings of the Throat Chakra being blocked. Not being able to be truthful, avoidance of confrontation and difficulty expressing wants and needs are also manifestations that the Throat Chakra is blocked and resonating a low and dull frequency.

When the Throat Chakra is overstimulated, there is a tendency to over share and be very vocal. Loud and abrupt conversations are frequent, and we have a tendency to interrupt conversations. We may start to notice that our inner circle of support becomes avoidant and

dismissive when conversing. We may cause anxiety within a crowd of
people as we may present as being unreliable and unpredictable.

- Here are some positive affirmations that support healing and
  anxiety management through the Throat Chakra:

- I am confident in what I have to say, and I am comfortable
  speaking my truth.

- I can express my needs and wants clearly and with confidence.

- I am in control of my voice, and I remain calm when faced
  with conflict.

- I am confident in communication within my relationships. I
  am honest and authentic.

6: See with Your Mind

The Sixth of the Chakras is called the 'Third Eye Chakra' with its
name in Sanskrit being 'Ajna'. The Third Eye Chakra is located as
the centre of the brow and is associated with the colour purple and
element of light. When researching the symbolism associated with
this Chakra, I was drawn to the Lotus flower with two petals with a
downward pointing triangle symbolising wisdom. Ever wondered if
you are clairvoyant? Do you hear the ringing in your ears? Are you
tuned into the spirit world? These are all associations with the Third

Eye Chakra. We may find that we have a strong intuition and we 'see' things with our mind. We have a clear perception of the inner and other world, with the angelic and the spirit realms alike.

When our Third Eye Chakra is healthy and balanced, we feel that we have a clear vision of the journey ahead and our inner vision is crystal clear. We do not let outside influences dull our clear vision. We can use spiritual techniques to clear away unwanted psychic attacks and our creativity and imagination flow easily, our moral compass is in tune on all levels, and we are open minded. To experience a blocked Third Eye Chakra, we would find ourselves having difficulty visualising the journey ahead, creativity is hindered, and we have feelings of emptiness and lack of perspective. We can feel dismissive of spirituality and experience closed mindedness.

Physically we can experience migraines and intense headaches as the energy is blocked and not flowing freely. Overstimulation of the Third Eye Chakra would manifest itself as the inability to concentrate and tending to jump to the worst-case scenario. We would be very superstitious and experience intense anxiety about the future. We would be ungrounded and out of control of thoughts and feelings, alongside being overwhelmed with life in general.

Here are some positive affirmations that support healing and anxiety management through the Third Eye Chakra:

- I trust my own intuition and I trust that my angels are guiding me.

- I am balanced in my thinking and my third eye energy flows in and out with ease,

- keeping it clear for me to see.

- I can concentrate on the tasks that I am doing, and I am in control of my thoughts and intuition.

- I am open minded and enjoy learning new things. My creativity and imagination flow with ease and I enjoy planning for the future.

7: Rise Up!

The Seventh of the Chakras is called the 'Crown Chakra' with its name in Sanskrit being 'Shasrara'. The Crown Chakra is located at the top of the head and is associated with the colour white-violet and element of source energy. When researching the symbolism associated with this Chakra, I was drawn to the Lotus flower with a thousand petals that represents infinity. This is the pinnacle of the mountain, at this point we are rising towards our higher power and have a connection with source energy. We are now at the stage of greater spirituality and enlightenment. At this stage, when our Chakra is healthy and balanced, we have a sense of true purpose in life. Life can be in harmony and there is true enjoyment and connection. We can experience a sense of meaning to life and trust that everything is as it should be. We feel unconditional love and protection from our higher power. We are truly willing to rise up and take the journey towards true connection.

If we are experiencing a blocked Chakra at this stage, we may feel uninspired and disconnected from life. Life may feel dull and boring with no joy or direction. We may have feelings of depression, loneliness and of being left behind and not being uplifted. We may take umbrage at being mocked for partaking in spirituality and believing in the higher powers which may lead to us being closed minded to the idea of a higher power. On the other hand, if our Crown Chakra is overstimulated, we may struggle with everyday life tasks. We may find that we are open to psychic absorption of other people's thoughts and feelings which may lead to being mentally unbalanced and disconnected from reality. Physical manifestation may show up as not taking care of the physical body and wellbeing and we may even stay out of the physical world.

Here are some positive affirmations that support healing and anxiety management through the Crown Chakra:

- I take care of my physical body as well as my spiritual one.

- I am grounded with strong roots and rising up to meet my higher power.

- I am comfortable mediating, listening to my intuition and I am confident in my spirituality.

- I am in control of my mind and can control psychic attacks.

- I trust that I am on the right path, and I am excited about what the future holds for my spiritual journey.

To End...

Well, the journey to empowerment never ends, it has only just begun. You have found a process where you can dip in and out, identify where your blocks are and how to heal them. This journey is not for the faint hearted but it is so uplifting and can give a sense of purpose. I hope my own story has inspired you, so you know that you are not alone in the struggles of life. I also hope that you have found this information helpful and wish to carry it forward to learn more. I am all about empowerment, so I have provided you with something you can use to get you to a place of feeling more in control. I have done my job.

Please feel free to reach out to me, I would love to hear from you. I have so many FREE resources that I would love to share with you. You can find me at www.thewhyterooms.com or email me at thewh yterooms@gmail.com

Sending so much love and light to you at this stage of your journey. Ruth x

Bibliography

I would like to thank the resources below who have inspired me from the moment I picked the book off the shelf, to finding the website that has inspired this chapter and my future course. Your information has been invaluable in leading me on this journey and supporting me though a time of darkness, leading me into the light.

1. Coleridge, G. (2018) The chakra project: How the healing power of energy can transform your life. London: Aster.

2. The chakras (2018) 7wisdoms.org. Available at: https://7wisd oms.org/chakras/ (Accessed: March 06, 2023).

Chapter Four

What It Really Takes

Michaela Edwards

"You won't ever make anything of yourself!"

That's what I was told aged 16 at Sixth Form. From that moment that voice became my imposter syndrome. For years I let the negative voice overtake everything. I didn't know what I wanted to do with my life because I felt like I wasn't good enough. At aged 18 I left collage with a B-tech in art and textiles and still no clue what I wanted to do. I took a full time job in a suit shop and realised very quickly I was very good at sales. I was able to up sell anything I wanted and soon became top sales on the shop floor. I learnt everything I possibly could about tailoring but my creative flare yearned for more. I LOVED dressing the mannequins and the window displays. I was always changing things up and moving things around. Soon after I was offered a Visual Merchandising role in London at age 20. Off I went with a very naive look on the world. I had no idea what I would encounter.

My first day in London was crazy! I was late for work after not being able to grasp the no queuing rule on the tubes and the trains. I wore high heels and soon realised why everyone was in trainers on the tube with flash suits! I rushed into Head Office feeling flustered and overwhelmed from the pushing and shoving and the closeness everyone stood on transport.

Things quickly picked up when I made friends with another VM and became close friends. She was from London so she showed me the sights and helped me settle into this new and crazy, fast paced life. She taught me how to be confident and stand up for myself.

I quickly fell in love with London. The buzz, the atmosphere after work. Bars and pubs were always buzzing no matter what day of the week it was. It was summertime when I first moved down and it just felt like I was Emily in Paris. Everything is better in the sunshine.

Four years passed and I met my now husband back home so a role was created for me back home where I covered the UK stores Visual Merchandising. In 2011 I was offered a Job as a visual merchandiser with PANDORA. I was to cover Yorkshire with my own company car. I was so excited I got my own car. I can remember the brand new black Mini clubman being delivered to my mum's house and thought I had made It in life. I loved my time at PANDORA. I grew from strength to strength and brought so many new ideas and procedures to the table. I designed a visual merchandising training programme to help train staff in stores so they could maintain displays in my absence as I had over 55 accounts so it was impossible for me to visit any more than on a monthly basis and you can imagine the state of the stores after a month with no VM assistance. This was rolled out to the entire UK. I also designed a window concept and a charm "tray layout" so each store had the same layout of charm trays to make it easier for customers to shop from store to store.

I left the corporate world when I was 26. A world of sales and visual merchandising, which I was really good at. I left to join my family business as a childminder and took over from my grandma who retired after 50 years in the business, which suited my family plans after getting married a month before and having my first daughter Scarlett in 2016. I threw myself into providing a fantastic service for my families and worked alongside my mum at her house until she retired in 2020 during the pandemic. This is when I quickly realised, I was an all or nothing kind of girl! During this time my grandma, who was also like another mum to me, had been fighting a terminal illness and she was sadly given weeks to live.

My Grandma was a strong lady and always there for everyone, she always put herself to the bottom of the pile so I was determined to be strong and not show any sadness during her final weeks. A few months before I had bought some materials to make some hair bows for my daughter Scarlett who was 18 months old at the time after struggling to find hair accessories that matched her outfits perfectly. I had made a couple and then shoved them in a drawer and forgot about them. I decided this would be the perfect distraction for me as my grandma deteriorated. I got some templates and a glue gun and began drawing round templates onto felt, hand cutting them out and gluing them together. I posted my work on social media and a couple of my friends commented wanting to buy some. Within a week I have sold 100 bows!

I sat down one evening and began drawing 100 bows out and started hand cutting them. 3 hours passed and I had only made 10 bows! Feeling so frustrated and deflated that I may not be able to make and sell these but determined not to give up before I had even started, I reached for my phone and started googling "how to make hair bows" and found a machine that cuts the material for you! My husband Grant bought me one and amazon primed it and I was holding my new machine the very next day! I tested it out straight away and it cut down my making time from 10 in 3 hours to 100 in 2 hours!!!

Once I got my first batch of bows out to my friend's word quickly spread, they post on their socials and their friends saw and came and ordered too. I decided I needed to start a page and give my business a name and it was on the 31 st March 2018 that Scarlett Emily's Bow Boutique was born! My grandma, Helen was a quirky and acentric lady! She loved glitter and sparkles. Whenever we went anywhere she used glitter hair gel in her hair and coloured hair mascara... remember those? I got some for Christmas in the 90's from the brand Groovy chic and my grandma was still using it in 2018! She LOVED body glitter too! The crazy thing is that she would have worn ALL of my hair accessories. She went to her local bingo a few nights a weeks and would clip tiny butterfly clips in her hair amongst the glitter and sparkle as they were her "good luck" charms. My beautiful grandma lasted just 10 days before she took her final breath and left us on 8 th April 2018. She did get to see the very start of Scarlett Emily's Bow Boutique (SEBB) I didn't give it up after she died, instead I threw myself into it and grew my page and my following over the next 12 months to over 3k followers! SEBB is and always will be my grandma's legacy!

In December 2018 I fell pregnant with my second daughter Annie. We decided to move house so I could childmind from my own home as Scarlett was also starting nursey soon and we wanted her to go to the nursery I delivered too as a childminder. Annie was born in August 2019 we named her Annie Helen – after my Grandma!

Orders were coming in thick and fast as the word of SEBB spread. My mum is as creative as I am so I roped her into designing, gluing, cutting, packing etc and she helped out on a weekly basis. I even got my dad on board with packing during the busier months too! I introduced a subscription box in October 2019 where customers paid £15 a month and got a gorgeous box of bows delivered to their door every month. I themed the boxes each month so the items complimented each other and were simply stunning. They were also exclusive so you had to buy the box to get the items. On my first month I got 28 subscribers! I trailed the boxes being a surprise, sneaking an item and revealing them completely. The reaction was very mixed but I found when it was promoted together and customers could see the full set they were more likely to buy into it. By July 2020 I was buying into 50 boxes to cover demand. In January 2020. I had got to the point where I couldn't get off my phone. I was constantly talking to customers about orders and selling product. And working 7am-6pm and a childminder with a new-born and a 3 year old was a real juggle. I was exhausted. I felt like I had no time for me or my family and the reason I chose to leave my career in VM was so I was there for my family.

So, I decided to move my business across to a website so customer could just order products without speaking to me. I rebranded and had a new logo designed and ordered branded backing cards which were a HUGE step away from my homemade kraft card backing cards I had currently been making, which saved me time making the cards too! I started introducing a few pre-made pieces onto the website to help ease the workload of "made to order" as none of my stock was pre-made in advance so I sourced some items from suppliers and started selling pieces that were already made. Launch was successful, and my following really supported the move to website. I was able to consolidate the subscription service too as shopify offered an app which took care of subscription payments for you, which again gave me some time back as I had to manually message everyone each month and ask for payments.

Then in March 2020 Boris made the announcement, we were going into lockdown! Me, my husband and two daughters were already on day 5 of isolation as Annie had developed a cough and testing wasn't available at that time. My childminding business closed overnight. As a self-employed woman I was scared! There was no furlough for the self-employed and it was such a scary time. For 7 weeks we ran as our little family unit with no income from my side. My husband was lucky as he could work remotely so he continued to work as he had before.

I am not going to lie, I went a little stir crazy with a 5 month old and a 3 year old during the first couple of weeks. I mean who didn't?! So Grant made it a rule that no matter what we were doing at 5pm we would down tools every day and go for a walk. We live super close to the Pennines so the walks are breath taking. I would put Annie in the sling and Grant would throw Scarlett on his shoulders and off we'd go. We live close to a golf course so we would walk across the grounds to get to the fields and hills. On the way there there was a bell golfers would use to ring to say they were about to swing. Scarlett loved ringing it every day. It was part of our route.

Lock down made SEB! Such a bold statement but its true! In May 2020 I took on my first team of brand reps. They were so excited, and some had been with me since the very beginning. Within a week my following grew from 5k to 6k on my main page and I tripled my income vs January 2020! Sales were coming in thick and fast. I was growing at a rate much faster than I had ever dreamt. Over the coming months we went from strength to strength. I took advantage of lockdown and held games nights on a Friday night, and I had such an amazing response! It created a lot of new customers and naturally generated the next phase of brand reps. My subscription boxes went wild too. I had to start ordering enough stock to make 50 boxes, the customers were just loving the monthly boxes dropping down. Success continued until the shops opened back up in July 2020 and then everything stopped. Fast. I dropped from £4k months to £1k months literally overnight. August was the same and I had invested in 50 subscription boxes and over half cancelled their subscriptions. It was a super tough month.

In September I decided to drop back down to 20 boxes whilst I built back up again. Sales started improving slowly as the novelty of being able to shop in actual shops wore off and I had a successful run up to Christmas, beating the previous year's figures by 30%! I decided to run some offers on black Friday week with a different offer every day. This massively helped get rid of old stock and saw us take £1k in one week which I hadn't seen since lock down. During the winter of 2020 I decided to grow my VIP group with my brand reps. I introduced "VIP brand rep take over week" where a brand rep took over the group for a week in exchange for store credit. They brought life and creativity to the group. Each rep sparkled with their own personalities and gave my community so much fun and excitement. My engagement went up by 150% and I gained so many new loyal customers. When I went for our next brand search I had so many people apply, and my team grew to 30 brand reps.

Over the next 12 months I rode a huge rollercoaster and I held on tight! It was like entering a theme park you had never been to before and choosing a ride. You had no idea what turns, drops or loop the loops would be thrown at you. You were scared and excited all at the same time. That's exactly what 2021 was for me. January is always quiet as everyone gets over Christmas, but we were booming in 2021 because once again we found ourselves in lockdown. The first quarter was a HUGE success so I took the decision to drop to wrap around care as a childminder so I could concentrate on SEB 9am-3pm every day. It was a big step and an exciting one too.

Fittingly my first day in my new format was on international women's day! When we came back out of lockdown in April 2021 things crashed overnight again. People were excited about being able to meet up again. Albeit in groups of 6 and outdoors but it was amazing, and everyone was excited. I mean me and my husband sat under an umbrella outside at a pub whilst it rained so hard the umbrella threatened to blow inside out but we did it because we hadn't been able too for so long! How many people did that? I meet with friends in gazebos with blankets and gloves to keep us warm and spent a pretty penny on bottles of wine just because we could. After not being able to do it for over 6 months it felt like a dream. So no wonder the world of online came to a halt.

It was bittersweet because SEB dropped over night but my childminding children began returning to me to counter balance my income. My mum had decided to retire during the first lock down and her children decided to move to my care so all the families I lost due to remote working were replaced by my mums' families. It took the pressure off us financially overnight. Especially as the market was so unstable for online retailers. In the September I gained new children for the new school year too. SEB started picking up again in October in time for the Christmas shoppers and I decided to repeat the offers I did on black Friday week the previous year. I took £1.5k in a week. I had so many orders I had to close my order books for pre-Christmas delivery immediately afterwards whilst I caught up.

It was here I decided I needed to become a fully pre-made business. Meaning all my products are made before I launch so they are ready to ship. This would mean I wouldn't have to close so early as I wouldn't be spending all my time making orders, I could just pack and ship them bringing turn around down from 3-4 weeks to just 1 week! It would also free me up to network and build my online presence. In July 2021 I found Mums In Business International or MIB, the biggest networking association aimed at women in businesses globally. I joined the main group and watched from a far, reading comments and taking so much value from these incredibly inspiring women. The CEO and founder Leona Burton is this incredible, powerful woman and showed us how to rock the business world whilst traveling and home schooling (then) 5 children. I was in complete awe of her!

Shortly after a lady named Becky Gilchrist jumped into my inbox asking me for a chat. I agreed and she spent 45 minutes with me discussing a plan and a goal for my business. She also told me to join "30 days to success" which was a free program Leona was running in January 2022. I had sat on the fence for so long with MIB not really participating but taking so much value. I was scared but I agreed and I signed up there and then. I remember setting my alarm on the evening of 1 st January 2022 ready for my first meeting with the 30 days to success program. I was filled with so much excitement and nervous energy. I barely slept. The meeting took place online on zoom at 6:30am for 30 minutes every day for 30 days. Just enough time before my childminding children arrived at 7am. I logged on and sat nervously in the waiting room waiting for the meeting to start. Leona let us all in and the meeting started. I watched the attendee numbers grow so fast as other women joined. There were 80 people on the call waiting to hear from the incredible Leona.

The meeting started and my hand couldn't move fast enough taking notes on everything Leona was saying. THEN the part I had been dreading happened! The break out rooms! Being thrown into a room full of women I didn't know filled me with dread. What if they don't see me as a woman in business? What if they laugh at my business and call it a "pipe dream", what if they think I am stupid? All these thoughts filled my head and I could feel myself spinning on the chair I was sat on. I didn't need to worry, the women were like a breath of fresh air! I was blown away! I was in that break out room for just 5 minutes and I came out feeling understood, empowered and brave. The adrenaline buzz after the first meeting was incredible. I decided to start couch25k again which I had attempted with a friend the previous year but gave up on week 4 when the shops opened back up again and choice retail over exercise... its where my heart truly lies. Anyway, I decided to begin the program alongside success to 30 days to keep me motivated and in line. Needless to say I completed them both within the 30 days! And oh my goodness what a start to the year! I met so many incredible women. A lot of which have become firm friends in the present day.

After 30 days to success, I attended my first ever networking meeting In Becky's MIB group. I was a spot light sponsor and Jan Oakenden was the guest speaker talking about the importance of mindset in business. I had been drawn to Jan in the 30 days to success. I had been in a couple of break out rooms with her and she was always snuggled up in an arm chair wrapped in a cozy dressing gown with her mass of curls piled on the top of her head. She had a super calming manner and has a lot of empathy in her voice. She is real and raw and I just loved that about her. She gave so much value I became her client instantly afterwards. Now me and Jan speak most days and she has become a really close friend. In February 2022 I decided to take the plunge and apply to become a MIB leader. There was a gap in Sheffield for a networking group so I decided to go for it.

After a call with Kye Burton I was offered the role of MIB leader for North Sheffield. I was given a brand-new group to build. This is where me and Jan became even closer as she was the leader for Leeds and Wakefield which was the next group to mine and only half an hour away so we chatted most days about what was working and what wasn't in our groups. 2022 was much like 2021 in the rollercoaster way of emotions.

In April 2022 I decided to invest in some new equipment so I could begin printing on water bottles, mugs, coasters etc. It's something I had wanted to do for a while, offering personalised gifts. I was super excited to get started, however an issue with a mug press set my anxiety going and I was filled with so much self doubt. I ordered a mug press that came highly recommended, I bought the mugs and the special printer so I was literally ready to go! The mug press arrived and it was faulty. I called up the company and the organised a replacement to be sent out, which came a few days later. The replacement mug press arrived with the same fault!! I was so frustrated as I just wanted to get started. So I called the company and they sent me ANOTHER replacement and assured me they would pick it out of another production line. It arrived a week later with the same fault AGAIN!!!

Feeling extremely frustrated I returned the 3rd press and demanded a refund. I popped a post on the MIB group asking for suggestions and loads of women came forward and said the particular brand I had picked were notorious for the fault I got but offered an alternative which was incidentally half the price of the original too! It arrived the next day and worked straight away so I was on a high thinking "yessss I can absolutely do this!" THEN I plugged my printer in and found it wasn't compatible with my MAC book. I tried everything and ended up having to use my husbands PC for it.

I found it really difficult to navigate the PC as I have had a MAC for over 15 years. So I called the company and they sent me software so I was able to upload to my MAC! Problem solved!! Or so I thought! I then printed my first sheet using the sublimation printer I had purchased and it was covered in printer lines. I tried everything and couldn't get rid of them. Feeling super frustrated and full of self-doubt I put everything in a cupboard and forgot about them.

In June 2022 I decided to take the plunge and try the equipment again with a clearer head. I cleared my day so I could focus just on the printer. I cleaned every nozzle, tip, ink jet you can think off. It took me all day but I DID IT!!! And by the end of the day I was holding my first perfectly printed mug! I was so incredibly proud of myself and my self doubt dulled. This spurred me on to create a full collection containing water bottles, mugs, coasters, travel mugs, tote bags, back packs and shoppers and launched a collection later that month! I STORMED teacher gifts and back to school water bottles, which became my best selling item pretty quickly. In the same month I decided to create an affiliate team with the reps that were loyal and supportive. Instead of handing out discounts, they received the commission instead! I started with 6 affiliates (Or consultants as we call them) and quickly grew to 30.

Within the first month I doubled my income on SEBB! Each consultant had their own FaceBook group and their own affiliate link. We discovered BOARDS, which as an app where you can upload all of your content straight to your keyboard and share it with your team so everyone has the correct content at their fingertips. This was an absolute game changer for us as it meant we were all on brand and shouting the same message. I met Siobhan Little who is an incredible Graphic Designer, through MIB and she popped some tile templates together for us on Canva too so we were able to create 1000s of pieces if content and upload it onto boards.

In September 2022 I got my biggest corporate order to date of 60 water bottles and 60 travel mugs for a company conference! I made the decision after this to open a second business to separate the hair accessories from the personalised goods. This is when All About Annie was born. It was in September I was also nominated for two awards at the first ever MIB INT awards and I won innovator of the year award! All About Annie is named after my second daughter Annie, my vision was to create bespoke gifts at affordable prices but as I launched, I got a couple of large corporate orders in so I began creating a corporate side to the business, offering businesses high quality merchandise for affordable prices with fast turn arounds and UK suppliers. So I began to make my presence in the corporate world.

In January 2023 I was approached by Leona Burton and asked to become the official supplier of the MIB INT merchandise, which was a huge honour. Off the back of becoming the official supplier I landed a vast amount of opportunities and created a drop shipping option on my website. Where a client wanting merchandise for their businesses can create a collection with their branding and then earn commission on each item sold. It means they don't have to invest in lots of stock as I print on demand and even cover the shipping. All the client has to do is sell!

My journey as an entrepreneur is just beginning really, I am learning so much every single day. But the key to success is connection connection CONNECTION!

Chapter Five

Embracing The Law Of Attraction For Success, Happiness And Growth

Emma Davis

A fter being in a corporate career for over 15 years, falling pregnant and not being supported in my current job role was a huge shock to my value and worth. I quickly realised that the 5:30am starts and 7:00pm finishes weren't going to work anymore and the career that I had worked so hard for would come to an end. During my pregnancy, I set up my business knowing that with my baby, I couldn't go back to that world.

I was already tired and exhausted from being pregnant, tipping lorries at 36 weeks pregnant, managing staff shortages and being an unsupportive manager. I had to fight for my position after my maternity leave to prove that I could work part-time as a manager because that wasn't the norm. All the while, I knew that I could do and be so much more. This drove me to keep working on setting up my business.

When I went back after maternity leave, I was back for 2.5 months when the unthinkable happened. I fell down the stairs carrying my baby. I thought my manager would care and be supportive but all he said knowing I was going to the hospital is 'who would look after the shop'? I knew that there was no going back. I couldn't return but still needed to scratch that itch of knowing that there was a career woman within me. This is when I fully threw myself into my events business. It would later grow into a marquee company.

FINDING THE LAW OF ATTRACTION

A change of scene brings up so much for us. I went on holiday to Mexico and sat there watching my daughter and ex -partner playing together, the weight of my life hit me like a truck. I was so desperately unhealthy, unhappy and overwhelmed that I knew that without drastic action I wouldn't see my daughter's next birthday. I don't know why but I felt the urge to speak to the universe. I asked the universe to show me what to do. 'Go on then, show me the way' and thought no more about it.

When I got home I saw an advert for mums in business and reached out. My first ticket was booked. I was struggling with postnatal depression and confidence was a struggle. There was so much doubt there about how I would do everything despite knowing that this career woman lurked inside. I went to my first mums in business meeting but was so anxious that all I could get out was 'Hi I'm Emma and I run a marquee company'. The guest speaker spoke about the law of attraction, and I thought 'this woman is batshit crazy'! She was talking about manifesting parking spaces, bringing in money and you are what you think. I sat there listening to her but I was so low and my life was pretty disastrous that hey, what did I have to lose, I just wanted to feel good again and happy. I'd tried everything else.

I left the meeting and drove home. I decided to go to a local store and on my way, I thought about that guest speaker. I thought about it and made the decision that when I got there, the one and only mum and baby parking space would be available to me. As I pulled into the car park the space was there waiting for me! What a coincidence I thought to myself. Surely there wasn't more to it than that. Then I decided to drive to another shop because I had to go and pick up some medication for my baby. The car park is always busy, it was raining hard but the parent and child spaces are never available. Ok, I thought, let's try this again. I drove around twice and someone pulled out of the space just as I turned the corner. Another parent and child space was mine! Wow, it happened again! I hate filling my car up with petrol, but

I couldn't avoid it any longer. I went to the self-service pumps and as I approached all 6 cars at the pumps pulled away. I could take my pick! I had never seen anything like this before.

We went home and Lacey went down for a nap. This is working I thought. I spoke to the universe again. I desperately needed £246 to pay the council tax bill or we would be in trouble. My phone started ringing and my ex-partner told me that he had a piece of work come in for.............£246.

PRACTICE MAKES PERFECT EVEN WHEN THINGS ARE HARD

I began to practice the law of attraction. I made the time to go sit and read 'The Secret' at a coffee shop on my own. I finished the book in one sitting and I wanted to know more and more and more. Things were starting to change. I was gaining more confidence and looking after myself, the business was making more money and I kept reading and learning everything that I could about the law of attraction.

Covid hit but things were still good. We had kept all of our bookings and I worked hard to keep an exceptional level of customer service in place. We kept all the bookings and moved them into the following year. I reassured brides who had booked us for weddings that everything would be ok and we didn't lose any of the work that we had gained. I felt lucky and positive that things would be ok.

I felt confident that the business would survive post covid, but I also recognised the opportunity to diversify. I wanted to share what I had learned with other women and mums so I trained as a life coach. I also gained qualifications in the law of attraction because this was something that had been so important to my journey.

Things didn't quite go to plan though. My marriage broke down and I became a single mum. This was a horrible and unexpected part of my journey. I don't know how I would have gotten through it if my mindset was as down and negative as it was in Mexico. I had come so far and even managed to stop my medication for postnatal depression. I wouldn't have gotten through any of it if I hadn't been practising what I know to practice.

I needed a break and some time away, so I manifested a trip to Spain. I had lost my home and didn't know what I would come back to. Of course, I manifested the perfect flat.

On a walk one day with my then-partner, I saw the most incredible fountains in a harbour. It was tranquil, it was beautiful, it was perfect. I said how beautiful it was and how lovely it would be to live there but my then-partner just dismissed it. I still remembered those fountains and my mum let me know when I returned from Spain that a friend had a flat available that overlooked them. I jumped at the chance. The perfect place for me and my little girl to be.

Part of living your best life and the law of attraction is letting go of the negative. I used journalling to get out the bad feelings and try to work through the actions of those who had hurt me. I didn't want to hold on to that hurt and that pain. I needed to release it and let it go to allow the incredible things to come next into my life.

BRINGING THE LAW OF ATTRACTION INTO YOUR LIFE

The law of attraction is now such a massive part of my life that I wanted to build a sanctuary of positive energy in my home. I decluttered my life and my environment. I got rid of all of those signs around my house like 'is it wine o'clock yet' or 'I don't want to be in the garden unless I'm drinking gin in it'.

I make myself a priority every day by getting out into nature, walking on the beach, meditating daily, and making vision boards with my goals and wishes as well as money mantras. These are free and easy things to bring into your world.

This has brought amazing people and opportunities into my life. I was able to run a 6-week course for mums at a local play centre, met a new business partner, remodelled my coaching, started a travel business and so much more. When negative things happen, I quickly get myself back into alignment by moving past them. I replaced the negative with positive signs all around me and you can do this too. Get rid of the negative messages in your environment and replace them with positivity.

LOST IN THE MAMARINTH

I love coaching women and mums. It lights my fire and I find myself in flow talking about the law of attraction and the positivity and opportunity that we can all be brought into our lives. I launched my new business 'The Happy as f**k club'. I had been meeting and supporting so many women who couldn't find their happiness and weren't making their own happiness a priority. Why shouldn't you be happy as f**k!

Often the only barrier is you. You don't feel worthy of happiness, you have a million excuses to avoid putting yourself first or you are so far removed from your own happiness that you simply don't know what makes you happy anymore. This is a depressingly common problem for women who are busy putting themselves bottom of the pile. Below their family, below their kids, below their partner, and even below the family dog. Prioritising your own happiness doesn't mean not loving or caring for your kids, but it also doesn't mean removing all the fun and happiness from your own life either. You deserve to be a priority.

I wanted to help all of these women become happy as f**K and started a coaching group with a monthly subscription. I quickly realised that I had undersold myself because I was worried that if the monthly cost was too high, no one would sign up. That self-doubt was creeping in but I thought that all I needed to do was share the membership more widely. That would work and then these women could be supporting each other even more.

To some extent I was right. Women in the group did support each other and sharing the highs of the journey was both motivating and affirming for everyone. Something just didn't feel right with the group though and I eventually announced that it would be closing. I was heartbroken that this business didn't work out because I felt that it was much needed and spoke to my soul but as a single mum, I also needed to make good financial choices about where I was putting my energy to pay the bills. Sometimes in business, we have to make hard decisions when our soul and the universe tell us that I am out of alignment. I had to be bold, brave, and close it.

I kept myself open to opportunities and I knew that the right one would find me. One of the women in my mums in the business group reached out to offer me the opportunity to work with her in her business. Jen was running a business called Mamarinth for mums who felt lost in the labyrinth of motherhood. Mamarinth started as an information business for local mums but issues with the post were making this hard. Jen was also suffering from the same issue in her business. She had tried to offer a group format at a low cost but that was just meaning lots of work for not much profit.

Jen and I chatted online about our businesses and realised that Mamarinth would be better served as a support and coaching platform for mums. I had drawn the right people and opportunities into my life because I was open to them and here it was. The opportunity had presented itself so that I could offer the coaching that I wanted to the women I felt I was most connected to and with the support of a business partner.

BE OPEN TO THE RIGHT COLLABORATIONS

Collaboration can be hard. Pick the wrong person and you'll make more work for yourself or ruin good friendships. Good collaborations are worth their weight in gold if you open up yourself to the input of the right people.

Jen and I have learnt how to work together and feed off of the strengths of each other for a shared vision. I am a great planner, creator and chatter. I have already spent thousands on training and courses to make myself the best coach and woman in business I can be. Jen is experienced at bringing courses and classes to life, building groups and ensuring that a business is progressing.

Between us, we quickly started to change the direction of Mamarinth to a shared vision. We created a 'Lost in the Mamarinth' Facebook group as a free community where mums can rant, share, support each other and find their tribe. The group has become the most incredible place to bring positivity into the lives of mums whilst acknowledging and sharing in the hard parts.

We ran our first Mamarinth Mums on a Mission Challenge as a 28-day model. Why 28 days? Because we don't want to be like other coaches who promise the moon on a stick. It takes time to form good habits and make real changes in your life but just like the Happy as F**k club we brought in a group format where women can support each other on their journey. Women supporting women and mums supporting mums were part of both of our groups that we could bring together. In 28 days women were making the most incredible changes and coming back to us after the course with examples of how they were continuing their journey to escape the Mamarinth.

MAPPING AND PLANNING

It's important to take the time to work out who you are speaking to. Jen and I sat down to map out what exactly was happening to mums and why. All of the women in our group had individual journeys but of course, we were seeing a huge amount of common themes and overlap. We sat down to map out the Mamarinth. Jen knows that I'm getting serious when the flipchart and coloured pens come out. Our styles might be different but when we collaborate we share the best of both of us.

The Mamarinth, we realised, has 4 pillars that keep women lost – Health & Well-being, Confidence, Time and Money. As coaches, we want to support women to look at all of these areas of their life together to make real change. Why have just a coach working on your career, if you're not confident enough to pursue it? Why start working on how you use your time if you don't have the money to outsource the things that you cant do? All the pillars of the Mamarinth need recognising, acknowledging and coaching together as women find their way out of the Mamarinth that has kept them so lost.

Utilising the law of attraction isn't just about thinking. What you write down and plan sends ripples out into the universe too. As we mapped out the Mamarinth we were naturally drawn to the women and mums who we could help the most. A lot of our clients have previously accessed all sorts of different support from medication to counselling but coaching has been so much more proactive and supportive as a way to make real change. Of course, we needed to bring this proactiveness and creativity into the mapping and planning of our business too.

WORKING WITH WOMEN AROUND THE LAW OF AT-TRACTION

When I am coaching women, I see them falling foul of a lot of the same common errors. Most people put a lot of barriers in their way straight away. They come to a coach and they want to talk about all of the things that are happening in their life, explaining the story and living in the now. We are conditioned to live out every aspect of what is happening to us, voice it, repeat it and live in the past. We find ourselves going backwards instead of going forward. The goal is to move clients towards letting go. You can't change the situations that have happened to you but you can change what you're doing to move forward, break negative cycles and vibrate on a higher frequency.

If you want to bring the law of attraction into your life, change the language that you're using. See them and believe them. Feel them physically and in your body because if your body is actually saying that you have fear around it, jealousy around it or anything. You won't be vibrating those positive messages internally and this will prevent you from manifesting what you want.

Resentment is a higher frequency than anger which is a common emotion for women and mums who have spent years or even decades at the bottom of the pile.

If you can bring yourself to a positive space, one day you'll be walking down the street just in awe of being alive. The sunshine, the positive people around you, and the flowers growing in the park will all be part of your consciousness rather than a constant stream of negative self-talk, messages, and misery.

People are living along either end of an imaginary stick. Some people are at the bottom, some people are at the top, and some people are working with way up or being challenged by the universe. We can dip down the stick but we can notice that and what affects us. For me, when I felt a dip, I noticed that moon phases and hormones are powerful so I can notice and block those days for respite and self-care in the future. Take the time to notice what impacts you and causes your energy to dip. This will help you not only in your life but in your business. When you're dipping isn't the time for a major business change or challenging yourself with a new project? It's time to step back, recuperate and recharge ready for the time when you're vibrating high and can jump back into your business.

The law of attraction is very much a journey that you need to go on, be open to and allow yourself to connect fully with yourself. The law of attraction is already in play regardless of what you're doing. Whatever is coming to you in your life is happening because of what you're putting out in the universe for good and bad. You will be able to look back with openness and see what you have created in your life and see what is happening because of your patterns, thoughts or self-sabotage. When I work with women they have an 'oh yeah, I can see where I am going with this. I can see what is happening here. If you're always on your partner's case, then they will keep doing things that will piss you off because that's what you expect. The same with your child's bad behaviour. We expect poor behaviour on that day out and what we expect we get whether it is conscious or unconscious. The law of attraction doesn't lie, it just is. Without sorting your vibration out so that you believe what you want to put out into the universe with your mind, body and soul, you won't be able to utilise the law of attraction.

Seeing women come through this journey and go from a spaced out, dead behind the eyes, lost soul, to someone with real sparkle inside and out is incredible and totally possible. The sparkle that you see from the women you admire comes from inside them and glows outside too.

START PRACTISING GRATITUDE

Start loving your own life. We get so into that tunnel of why life is crap, our partner is crap, our business isn't where we want it to be and we're stuck in the fogginess of doom and gloom. Turn around and look at the life, business, and relationships that you have created. Be grateful for what you have.

We can change the people around us with gratitude without having to have family or business arguments and showdowns. If you expect that your partner won't support, you in growing your business then you'll get what you expect. You're putting these messages out into the world and you're getting them back.

I don't really hit red lights, traffic or other barriers because I am grateful and open to things going well in my life. I don't get rained on during the school run when Jen (only 4 miles away) repeatedly get's drenched every day. Now it's a running joke and the more that we laugh about it, the more that rains pours down on her whilst I am bringing the warmth and sunshine.

When you're running late for a meeting, stop the negative self-talk about the traffic. Stop telling yourself that you won't find parking or that it's a waste of time. Be grateful and positive about the day ahead and watch the universe deliver for you. Don't engage in negative self-talk with others either. If someone is putting you down or giving you limiting beliefs about your business then they should not be in your tribe. Your tribe should be full of your top supporters and people who are rooting for your success. Practice gratitude when you're talking to others about yourself, your life and your business with positivity and love. You can't practice gratitude during negative self-talk.

You can surround yourself with gratitude through your positive messages. Stick up signs and photos around you of what you are grateful for and celebrate the gratitude of others. Don't put those thank you cards from clients in the bin. Celebrate them in your workspace to create positive vibes around you. Allow yourself to celebrate the positive impact that you have on others.

BE RUTHLESS WITH WHERE YOU DIVERSIFY

I love taking on new businesses and new challenges but if something doesn't feel good then don't do it. There is a difference between negative self-talk that holds you back and the universe telling you that something isn't working for you. Listen to it, thin out what you're doing and move on. It's easy to find yourself adding new businesses, new services, new products, or something totally different. Be careful where you are spending and aligning your energies. If you find yourself spending your time on tiny pockets of work you may find that clients expect the moon a stick for their low cost, two or three hours of work and you spend more time talking about, worrying about and thinking about the tasks and the difficulties than you do commit yourself to quality clients and work where you can make real change and find real success.

Overstretch, burnt-out people can't be high vibe, find happiness or utilise the law of attraction because they are too thick into the fog of their life and their business to be grateful for what they have. Adding a new thing won't necessarily make your life or your business better but it may come at a great financial or emotional cost. How many women have spent a fortune on classes, courses and training that they don't use? How many women have started small businesses but are unable to fully commit themselves to them to find success? How many women have thousands in stock or kits sat in a garage somewhere as a dusty, unused pipedream? People are happy to offer you the alleged solution to your problem but it's not a solution or an opportunity if it makes your life harder.

Aim to surround yourself with ease, success, and abundance. It is better to find organic growth and celebrate the little wins in your business than it is to berate yourself for opportunities you missed that you never had the time or energy for anyway.

Not everything that you are involved in needs to be a business. I may love a makeup brand but I don't need to be a rep, I may love a nutritional supplement but I don't need to be a rep. Or I can sign up and know that this is something for me to make a residual income but doesn't need to become a massive business. You can't do every business all the time. You won't have enough time or energy to go around. Find what makes your heart and soul sing and move towards that but do it in a way that you can be grateful for what is coming into your life and the opportunities that come with it.

YOU DESERVE GREAT THINGS

Believe that you deserve great things and this is what will come to you. I believe that we are all capable of and deserving of great things and I believe and want this for you too. You just have to believe it and want it for yourself.

Chapter Six

Take Risks And Don't Just Settle!

Nicola Peake

E asy for me to say, I am running a business I love. Look at my socials, I am out and about, hosting fun events such as spa days, lunches, cold water swims, and spending time with other fabulous business owners. So, who am I to tell you to not settle? Well, that may all sound incredible, and starting my chapter in this way may sound a bit wanky, but stick with me, it hasn't always been this way.

Over 40 years in the making.

I was an only child growing up, it was only me and my Mom (I am a Brummy and this is how we write and say it - I make no apologies) Anyway, although I had a very loving home, I was lonely. All my friends had siblings and "proper" families and I had Sonic the Hedgehog and the radio. We all remember taping the charts right?? I didn't have anything to do with my Dad, he spent most of my childhood in prison. He would occasionally come over and show his face, but there was no relationship there. Throughout my younger life I guess I was always craving connection. Back then, it was seen as attention seeking. I was always the loudest of my friends, I wanted to be involved in everything and I hated missing out.

I felt like I never really fit in with everyone else. I went to good schools, and my friends all had nice houses, their parents had nice cars, they went on school trips and family holidays. I grew up on a Council estate, my Mom didn't drive, I don't remember asking to go on school trips and our holidays would be to blackpool. (I loved it!) The friends who knew from where I lived soon turned on me when I started senior school, to them I was the posh kid because I didn't go to the local school, so I didn't fit in there either, I would be picked on walking home almost daily.

So, by the time I was 12, I had experienced loneliness, rejection by my Dad, comparisonitis, feelings of not fitting in and my confidence and self-worth wasn't great. No one would believe that, because I dealt with it by being the loud one, I was confident and gobby from the outside, but anxious on the inside.

During my school years things happened which made me feel different and unaccepted, such as being made to sit at the front of my R.E class, by my Nun teacher for being a Bastard! Yes, she really did that. I was picked out and bullied by a Nun, because my Mom wasn't married, and she announced to the whole class that it was because I was a Bastard! I was left out of things by friends, things which now would seem ridiculous to worry about, but to me back then, they were huge. Rejection was a big thing for me, so when those closest to me did it, it really hurt and stayed with me for life.

As I got older, I just loved being around people, and once I was 16 I decided to leave school and work for a hotel as a waitress. I was never as clever as everyone else, and sixth form and university were never on my agenda. I just wanted to work, meet more people and earn my own money.

The Cycle Breaker

Where I lived, most people my age were all following similar paths. Drugs and violence or having babies and claiming benefits, or both, and this was not the life I wanted. My Mom had always worked hard, and she set a great example to me, not like my Dad. I didn't want the type of life my Dad lived. I had a choice, I could have easily gone down a different path with a group of people I mixed with, or I could work hard, meet new people and create a different life. Thankfully I chose the latter - seeing them beat a lad with baseball bats, because he wasn't from the same postcode, led me to never see these people again. This was not the path I wanted to go down.

I loved working at the hotel, I worked as many shifts as I could, and my social life was brilliant. As I got older, I started to want a "proper job" . I had met someone, and although I was still incredibly young, I wanted to grow up, settle down and earn more money. I was fortunate enough to land a job in a bank of all places! Me, who got an E in Maths, was now working in a bank! By the age of 20, I had a mortgage, a baby, lots of new friends, and I was settled into a new career.

I was the cycle breaker.

The Pursuit of What??

I always wanted to do well, and all through my working life I felt like I needed and wanted more. If only I had worked on my mindset at 18 and not 42! As soon as I started working for the bank, I was inspired by those who were earning more, those who had good sales jobs and the company cars. So, you guessed it, I wanted that too. I had my gorgeous daughter Georgia who I wanted to give everything to. I wanted her to have everything I thought was important, and didn't have growing up, so I worked so hard to progress. By 25 I was a qualified financial adviser. I had started to set myself up for a lovely secure life, but I sabotaged it.

I now wasn't happy in my relationship, I wanted what I thought was more excitement, more adventure in life and I was always looking at either new houses, holidays, cars, buying random items in my lunch

breaks (I now have a 20 year old armchair which I bought for £1000
- and no I didn't need it, and I still don't!) and I never really knew
why. I think now it was just for that instant rush of satisfaction. My
reckless behaviour expanded into relationships, making many ridiculous mistakes, believing that they would always bring me more, more
happiness, stability, fun. I really don't know "what" if I'm honest, but
I just craved more. In truth it brought more pain, hurt, mentally and
physically, not only to me but to Georgia, my friends and family. I
ended up in a lot of debt, I bought and sold houses during the boom,
and still come out the other side with negative equity. My pursuit of
always wanting more led me to having less. My 20s were a bit chaotic
to say the least, professionally I was stepping up the career ladder, but
I just didn't know how to deal with it and manage myself. I look back
now and believe this was down to my very low self-worth.

Growing up...maybe?

At 28 I met Rob, and at 30 we had Daisy, and finally I had stability
and happiness. Of course I was still in the pursuit of more, more
money, more freedom, and after a few years I decided to leave my
secure employed job and go to work for a practice, self-employed.

THIS WAS IT!!

I had freedom, I had a great income, our debts were almost clear.
We had amazing holidays, I had a great car, I was striving to provide

my family with everything I could. However, I was still doing crazy things, overspending, making impulsive purchases - like buying a 26 foot above ground swimming pool one day! (it was a bloody pain in the ass by the way). When Georgia turned 18, I had a car delivered with a big red bow and a private number plate. She said to me a few hours later 'Mom, you don't need to keep trying to give me what you didn't have'. She was right, and way more sensible than me. I was still, at 38, trying to make sure we had all the nice things, and that we would fit in. I told myself it was for them, but was it really? because let's be honest, who was it helping? Me, it was all about how it made me feel, and these big gestures, and overspending, made me feel better.

As you can probably tell, I was never a great saver! I was bloody great at advising others, but I never took my own advice. I was now paying into my pension and planning ahead, but I lived each day as it came. I believed I was in the last leg of my career, and that my business would just continue to build in value. I was in ignorant happy bliss, and I had no idea what was coming....

The Final Straw

Early January 2020 I found myself out of work for the first time since the age of 15. 12 months earlier, the business I believed I was building was gone, the practice owners decided to sell up, and this left me right back at the start, losing all the recurring revenue I had built. The shock of this, and the deceit sent me into an awful place mentally. The income I was so used to receiving stopped, which led to the build up of debts, and then after 12 months of hell, pursuing what I was entitled to, and failing, I was managed out. We were in a mess. I visited the job centre, to be told that I wasn't entitled to anything. I applied for jobs which I didn't really want, because we needed the money. I spent every day on the phone to recruiters and I was deeply depressed. There were a few nights where my husband would hide the keys, so I couldn't leave the house, as the river was more appealing to me, than facing the failure I was.

I don't need to tell you what comes next! Covid! Now I couldn't get a job, recruiting ceased, everyone was at home and we were stuck in limbo.

The Lightbulb Moment

It sounds a bit cheesy, but there did seem to be a switch inside me which made me realise just how unhappy I had become, and I knew it was time to give up the career I had worked so hard to build all my life. I started to think about what I could do instead. I loved food, cooking, baking, so this was where my mind was going. I had always dreamt of running my own small restaurant or wine bar, but obviously this wasn't on the cards as 1) I had absolutely no money, and 2) they were all closed!

Remember those lovely hot days during lockdown? Well, one of those days, I was sitting in the garden with a glass of wine, reading a magazine, and I saw a picture of an afternoon tea! Lightbulb Moment!

I went straight to facebook and asked if people would be interested if I made up Afternoon Teas and delivered them to their door, safely of course, and the response was amazing. A week later, I was trying them out and delivering them to friends and family, and then I started advertising online. I created business pages on all the social sites, applied to all the right departments, so that I could sell food from home.

After a few weeks, I was receiving orders through facebook, and I was delivering gifts for people who couldn't see each other. I loved it. I then got offered a job! Ahhhh, what do I do? My friends said I should take it, they told me to be sensible, it's a secure regular income, and I could always carry on the hobby on the side... But this was more than a hobby to me, this was the start of a new exciting business. So I took the risk, and turned the job down.

Chouxlicious went from strength to strength. It wasn't easy, and as soon as I started advertising on my socials, more and more local businesses started to offer the same, so I had to think bigger! Why keep my services restricted to where I live? So, I decided to offer National Deliveries. The first few trial deliveries were disastrous, but I kept going until I perfected it! December 2020, we were put back into lockdown, and from then, the business just flew. January, I turned over 20k, February 15k, March 20k....... Everyone was sending gifts, Valentines, Mothers Day, Birthdays, Anniversaries. I found a demand and made the most of it. I was in magazines, including BBCs Olive Magazine, I was listed next to Rick Stein as one of the best delivery companies in the U.K, and I was receiving order after order every day!

Oh no.......

Fast forward to July 2021, and the business was still thriving. The orders reduced a little, I was averaging 10k a month, BUT, the world was opening up and I was stuck in my kitchen every day packing boxes. I still couldn't see anyone, and I was missing people. My whole life I had worked with people, and I was now alone, every day, and I started to resent my business. I ploughed on, but I would dread any new order, I would be really fussy over enquiries for weddings and events because I didn't want to lose my weekends, especially when I was so alone all week. I had to start to accept that the business I loved, which was my baby, and which I was so so proud of, was not putting the fire in my belly anymore. But what the hell do I do now??

I knew I was NEVER going back to working in a corporate environment again, and I definitely wasn't employable! I had to create a business which I would not get bored of, I needed to be around people, and I needed to be out and about and not stuck in my house every day.

Let the crazy ideas commence.....

I refused to settle.

I won't lie, I did not want to just let Chouxlicious go. I had put my heart and soul into it, and it had changed my life!

I was also so worried that I would look like a failure again. I cared far too much about what people would think about me closing the business. Would they think I wasn't making money anymore? Would they think it had all gone wrong? Would they think it was just me going through a fad? Would they think I was unsuccessful? This crippled me for a good few months, so I just kept going. I wasn't miserable, but I was just ploughing through each day.

The big thing which helped me at this time, were the amazing new people I had met online. You see, during lockdown I turned to social media, it was this whole new world full of people like me, people who wanted more, who were working their ass off to give themselves a better life. They were all building their own business, and they understood what I was feeling. They were there when I was low, and they celebrated my wins, there was no judgement. I was making new friends and new connections, and I couldn't wait to meet them in real life and give them a squeeze! This is where my ideas started to grow from.

I loved people. I wanted to get back out and meet new people. I wanted to be able to do nice things. One of the perks of the corporate world were the great things we got to do, from the staff nights out, to trips abroad. We would enjoy time together doing nice things, and when you have your own business, these things don't happen anymore. No more leaving do's, no more incentives or team events. It is now just us, and if you're anything like I was, you don't allow yourself time off to do these nice things. You feel guilty when you are not working on your business, and you don't incentivise yourself, or treat yourself to a nice day out.

I thought about networking to meet new people in person, this way I would still be working on my business, and I would be out meeting new people. However the thought of it filled me with dread. I always hated networking, you know the ones, 6am starts, 60 second pitches, and pinstripe suits! I looked around for some different events, somewhere where I would find people who didn't just want to sell, but wanted to make real connections. I wanted to find something different than a boring hotel room, I wanted nice surroundings, good food, nice locations and a bit of luxury, and I couldn't find anything at that time, so you guessed it, I decided to create my own!!

This was it! I could create amazing events for female business owners. These events would be fun, real, and give everyone the time to really get to know each other. No pitches, no sleazy selling, just genuine connection. I could plan more luxurious events so that we would also treat ourselves for the hard work we put into our business. I could offer these to all of the amazing people I had met online, and I could connect them all, as well as meet them and have a great time! This is where my idea for Peakes Private Members Club was born. This was August 2021, Peakes didn't open until December!

I didn't know whether to run both businesses alongside each other, I didn't want to just let go of Chouxlicious, so I battled with myself for months. Like I mentioned before, I was so worried that people would think I had failed, until I was given a great piece of advice.... "When we learn to ride a bike, it takes time. We keep trying until we perfect it, we make mistakes, fall off, but we keep going. We then ride the bike really easily, and we know exactly what we are doing. As we grow, we realise that we have outgrown our first bike, and we want a bigger, better one. That was our practice bike and now we can go for the real one"

This is what had happened with Chouxlicious. It was my first, I learned how to set up a business, I had my practice run and nailed it, and now it was time to move on to the next bigger business which I would love even more and keep forever. If you have found yourself running a business which no longer lights you up, and you have experienced the same worries as me, just look at it in this way. You are learning all the time, growing, ready to move on to the next bigger and better business. Do not Settle.

A New Start

December 2021, I decide to just go for it! In between all of my Christmas orders, I was working hard on mapping out what my new business would look like. I decided I needed to create a community, I wanted to bring people together, and make them feel that they were a part of something. I opened Peakes Private Members Club properly in between Christmas and New Year, and by the 1st of January I had over 30 new members. People could see what my vision was, and trusted me to be a part of my community. Within a few months I had 100 members, and I started to plan and host the fabulous events. I closed my diary for new orders and Chouxlicious was now for sale.

There was no way that I could run both businesses. I had to go all in with Peakes to make it a success, and that was the next best decision I made. Chouxlicious is now in the hands of a lovely new owner. Today, Peakes has been running for over 12 months and I have absolutely loved every second of it. I have hosted 14 events across the U.K, we have enjoyed lunches, spa days, comedy clubs, cold water swims, as well as a gorgeous retreat in the highlands. This year the events will be even bigger and better, and one day I would love to create one big inspirational business event.

I never get bored. I am surrounded by amazing people, and I get to be out, meeting people every month. I also love attending other people's events, there are so many people who are creating amazing experiences, which are all brilliant ways for us to meet new people and build new connections. Is it time for you to stop settling?

I set up both of these businesses with absolutely nothing. I didn't have savings in the bank, and my husband's income went on all of the bills. So, if you are telling yourself that you will wait until you have 'x' amount in the bank, it will probably never happen! I appreciate how hard it would be to leave a secure job, to risk it all to not settle, and to chase your dream which you know will make you happy. If I didn't lose my job, would I have done any of this? Would I have chosen to give it up, to follow my dream of working for myself? I honestly don't know, but I do know that I am so glad it happened, and I am so glad I didn't just step back into another job. I followed my dream and trusted in myself.

You may be thinking, how do you start! How do you just set up a business and make it a success? Well first of all - don't overthink it! I see so many people who work and work and work on setting up their business. They want the fancy website, they want their branding to look amazing, they invest in course, after course BEFORE starting to sell. They feel that everything needs to be perfect first. This is not the case! Yes, invest in yourself and keep learning, but make sure that you are selling and bringing in the money first. Once you start to build up your income, then spend money on the nice to haves.

Don't compare yourself to others. It is good to take a look at your competitors, but do this for inspiration. There will always be people who do what you want to do, and have done it longer. There will always be people who are more successful, but this should never make you stop following your own dream. There will also be plenty of people who will be looking up to you. Be inspired and inspire others. Ignore the negative nellies! You know the ones, they will only see the downside in every plan you make. You may have people around you, who love you but will feel threatened that you want to be successful, they will tell you that you are making mistakes, because they want to keep you where you are now, as it keeps them safe.

Find the right people! You have probably reaslised by now that I am a big advocate for people having the right connections. Connecting with the right people will help keep that fire in your belly ignited. The power of having a support network is priceless. Join communities on social media, attend events and interact and engage online. Allowing yourself to be open to meeting new people is key. Get to know them, listen to them, take an interest in what they have to say to you. Just as you would build a friendship in the 'real world', build friendships and connections in the business world too.

Word of mouth is invaluable when welcoming-in new clients. Having someone 'vouch' for you can be the difference between making the sale or not. The larger your circle or network, the larger your potential market. If I hadn't expanded my circle and worked on building relationships as much as I could, I wouldn't now have 125 amazing business women in my membership after a year of launching. Get comfortable being uncomfortable.

Building a business is not easy and there are so many parts to running a business which is uncomfortable. I used to worry about posting on my personal Facebook page for example, because it's so public, I would worry about what my friends and family would think. I would worry about what other business owners would think, but over time, when people started to engage with me, join my membership, and become friends, it became so much easier and now it's something I do easily every day without any worries at all.

So do the things which make you feel uncomfortable, be consistent, be proactive and in time, I promise you, you will see the rewards and feel the successes.

Take Action

Imposter Syndrome can play a huge role in our lives, whether personally or in business. The voice inside that tells us we 'aren't ready', 'aren't good enough', that we need more experience and so on is a bugger! It's there, within our subconscious, to keep us safe from potential threats, but what is the worst that will happen when you take action in your business? It will feel terrifying at times to take that step out of your comfort zone, but that's the only way you are going to reach your goals. Taking action is key in the success of your business. If you sit there, staying comfortable and waiting for things to come to you, you are effectively 'leaving money on the table'.

This year I have made myself a promise to do the things which make me want to run for the hills. I am speaking on stage - something I said that I will never do. I am being more visible, launching new things which I have sat on for months, and I am just going to give things a go. If I make an idiot of myself, then so be it! The thing we often don't realise when setting-up a business, is that mistakes are just as valuable as something going right. It may not lead to the outcome you're hoping for, but it's experience which will help you to do things better next time around. So try not to let a fear of failure hold you back - the only true failure would be not ever trying to make a success of your business. Make a promise to yourself today, that you will choose to not settle. Life is for living, you deserve to be happy and live the life which makes you happy.

What is my long term vision?

I'm not going to lie, I want to earn a lot of money. I want the financial freedom I have always craved. That doesn't necessarily mean I want lots of money to buy a big car, house, holiday or designer goods, although I wouldn't say no! Freedom to me is to have no debts, to be able to do impulsive things like nights out, weekend breaks, treat my family, and to keep investing in myself and my business. I want to be in a position where I don't need to check my bank balance before a shopping trip or holiday.

I want to build Peakes to 250 members, and help create hundreds of amazing new connections. I want my own network to grow, and I want to take every opportunity I can to build my own business, profile and connections. I want to inspire and help hundreds and then thousands of people to follow their passion and their dreams. Life is too short to be in an unhappy workplace, or to be working all hours running a business you resent.

You deserve to be happy, for you and for everyone around you, so let me ask, what can you do now to make your life happier and not settle?

Chapter Seven

Carving Out Your Own Path To Success

Jen Fisher

T his was never my plan.

I never thought that I was meant to run a business.

Yet here I am. Carving out my own path full of little moments and monumental ones.

Over the past 2.5 years I have learnt to carve out the wins, bulldoze over the loses and barriers and not to ever backdown. It's brought me financial security, flexibility around a lot of the school runs, the ability to throw myself into full time business and the odd award to. I am a firm believer that anyone can carve out their own path if they want to. I always admired those who had a business they were passionate about but I grew up with a very clear path that would propel my career into Local Authority life straight out of University. I spent the next fifteen or so years zig zagging my way from job to job, from department to department believing that life was 9-5, or more accurately 8-5 if I wanted to get a parking space.

Logically I knew that inequality was something that affected women but I didn't really get it until it was thrust in my face. My body was changing, my life was changing, the way I saw the world was changing... I was pregnant and the way the world treated me had shifted forever. I wasn't even unexpectedly pregnant. I took the typical path. Steady job, marriage, pregnancy. Yet, it sent shock waves through my life as it does so many women. I tried to find myself again, I really did. The me that existed before pregnancy, before birth trauma, a special care baby, 3am feeds and postnatal anxiety and depression but she just didn't exist anymore.

There was no going back. I longed for more and I couldn't fit into that Local Authority box that I had called home for so long. That career path filled me with dread. I was utterly sick of disappointing everyone around me by not bouncing back a previous version of myself. For being torn in a million directions. It was time for a change! I carved out my own path and you can to.

FINDING THE RIGHT PATH

Throughout my career I had worked with businesses and as I drove to houses with swimming pools in a Nissan Micra with a broken wing mirror and huge childcare bill, I felt increasingly strongly that I could do it to. There was nothing particularly special about the businesses I saw, only that they knew their industries well and were happy to flow with the good and bad times. I felt more than a little lost as to what I would do. I have no natural crafting talent, I'm not particularly into health and beauty, I shouldn't be trusted to cut anyone's hair and didn't have any budding hobbies that I could monetise. In that regard I would say that I was at a distinct disadvantage to many that I knew! If you love doing your nails or sew your own clothes then it's easy to start building a business on that passion. I loved business, but had no idea what business would be right for me. If this is you, don't panic. The right venture will find you. What do you love? What are you good at that others aren't? What could do a talk on?

Now 2.5 years into my first serious business I know the power of putting what I want out into the universe but at the time I had no idea how to make things happen aside from applying for a better job in the same organisation. I had started to dream of running my own business and the universe plonked the idea straight into my lap. A Facebook ad to run baby and child first aid classes for families kept appearing during my Facebook scrolls. Yes, I thought, that could be me, I could do that. Suddenly it just felt like the right fit.

This is where I learnt about carving out my own path and I've continued with this concept ever since. Carving out my own path, carving out success, carving out time and carving out little moments of calm. I learnt quickly that we are all in the driving seat of our own life if we stop coasting. If your life or your business isn't where you want it to be, the good news is that you're in control. It's scary but it's true. I had to learn to let go of caring what other people think and the voice that told me I was crazy to go ahead. If you don't believe in your business then one else will. It starts with you. So, I did it. I jumped online, made calls, sent emails and landed on Mini First Aid.

YOU DON'T NEED PEOPLE TO BELIEVE IN YOU.

You don't need the people around you right now to support or believe in you to start or move forward. Plenty of people in my life told me not to start a business and to stay in my lane. That steady little Local Authority job was my speed they said, not business life. I would surely fail. Despite me being unhappy, unfulfilled and in an unworkable situation a lot of people tried to dissuade me from my plan. I believed in me though and that was all that mattered. I ploughed forward regardless. Eventually I found my mums in business tribe and now I have that army of amazing women behind me. You can build a network from scratch. People may be invested in trying to keep you small because if you succeed it will be confronting to them. If you succeed they will wonder why they couldn't or you might out grow them. Screw them! Keep carving out your own path regardless.

In October 2019 I bought my franchise, then called Mini First Aid East Sussex and only providing baby and child first aid classes for parents/carers. Now 2.5 years later I've been on an incredible journey to expand to Mini First Aid Sussex and offer classes for the whole family. I spent the next 6 months updating my training and preparing to launch my franchise as I was also still in my day job and had an 18-month-old. My original launch date was April 2020 and you can imagine how that went!

CARVE A PATH AROUND THE BUMPS

I remember sitting in a paediatric first aid class in late March 2020 as Covid hit the UK. I drove home having passed the last piece of training I needed, the sun beaming through my car windows. I lapped up the sun hitting my face and turned up the volume on the radio. That was the last time I would leave the house for 12 weeks. I was deemed clinically vulnerable and told to isolate. I pulled my daughter out of nursery, my launch was cancelled and I spent three months trying to manage a challenging social care job at home with an 18-month-old drawing on the tables, screaming when I was on the phone and needing to be put down for a nap in the middle of a team meeting. I could have given up at this point but I was determined to carve out my own path. I had all the qualifications and kit to launch my business and here was an opportunity to do something good at a time that people needed it, and make extra money for my family.

I started to advertise my first classes on Zoom and covered a few classes for others to. My early classes for my own business were a bit floppy in those first strange lockdown months. Some had no sales or were cancelled, others were mostly being done for free with local businesses for promotion, some had one person attending. I simply kept going. I asked for anyone attending to give me a review and share the class with others. I sent out certificates so photos could be shared on other businesses social media. This was the start of me learning the power of networking which has been an essential pillar to the success of my business. These times were challenging mentally, physically and financially but I was able to use this bumpy period to set myself up for success. I kept attending online networking events, posting on my social media, introducing myself to complimentary businesses over messenger and commenting on local relevant posts. I believed that my business couldn't possibly be over before it began. I simply refused to let that happen and continued to carve out my path forward.

BULLDOZING THROUGH ROUGH TIMES CAN SMOOTH THE FOUNDATIONS FOR THE GOOD TIMES

I'd been putting in the work and laying good foundations in the solid belief that my business could and would succeed. My first in person class sold out and I was able to use the online skills I had learnt during the first lockdown to ride out the next two waves of Covid. Yet, many businesses collapsed during this time when mine not only officially launched but flourished and rapidly grew. The sheer force with which I continued to hit the market, hit social media and shared my passion worked. I carved out the path that I wanted by telling my story and sharing why I felt that my class was one not to be missed. Don't ever try to diminish that passion or fire in your belly for your business or for the life that you want to create. Let it out! Let people see it when you talk about your business, let people see it on social media, let people see it when you excitedly tell them about your achievements over coffee.

In April 2021 I took on the role of head leader for the Eastbourne, Bexhill & Hastings Mums in Business group in East Sussex. I think that it is so important that women, particularly mothers have the confidence to continue to carve out their own path. There was irony that I would see time and time again in the group. Motherhood was often the time that women were starting a business because life had changed, the workforce had become more complex, they were being crippled with childcare costs or they simply wanted a different type of life. Yet......this was also a time when many lost their confidence and lacked direction. They didn't want to go live on social media or stand up as the face of their business because they weren't confident or just didn't like the way they looked when they saw themselves scrolling through their phone. When their businesses weren't going well and they weren't seeing results this knocked their confidence further.

Each and every one of those women could stand up and be counted if only they could find the confidence within themselves to bulldoze through barriers and carve out the life and the business that they want. We have a saying in our Eastbourne, Bexhill & Hastings Mums in Business group. Rev that bulldozer! Don't sit back and moan. Get into the market and show everyone who you are, what you do and why they should be buying from you. Sales looking a bit low? Rev that bulldozer! Get your game face on and go for it. No one ever made a successful business without showing that they passionately believe in their product/service and having people to talk to about it. Whatever you're doing, do with gusto and carve out the path that you want for yourself and your business, unapologetically and with passion and fire.

LOST IN THE MAMARINTH

My businesses have enabled me to meet some incredible women in business but many have the same story. They didn't intend to be in business either. This wasn't their plan, like it wasn't initially mine even if it was a new path that I was carving out for myself. Many had employment and moved into business after returning from maternity leave to find that the world of work just didn't treat them the same and they were worn down to the point that they simply couldn't take anymore. They had to make changes and so did I. There I was balancing my busy albeit part time day job with evening and weekend first aid classes. Something had to give.

I came alive in my business which allowed me the proactive ability to make real changes and be creative in a way that my day job didn't fulfil and I was finding the world's view of me as a mother difficult to comprehend at a time when in my business, I was achieving more than I ever had done before. My business was growing but my employed self was a shrinking husk of what I had been. I used to feel that fire in my belly for my day job but now I just felt exhausted, overworked and underpaid. I had reached the tipping point where my business was demanding more and more of me, toppling into every aspect of my life. So, I did it. I quit my job. The day I quit my job I asked my Mums in Business Eastbourne, Bexhill & Hastings group for support.

Please don't let this fail I begged them. Don't let me fail. I need this to fly like it has never done before so share on social media, give out leaflets and talk about what I am doing with these classes. A lot of women in business that I meet seem strangely unable to ask for and get what they want. In fact, one of my friends who was looking to start her business said to me "Jen, you always get what you want" as if maybe this was a bit of a bad thing??? Why would it bad to directly ask for what I want and need? To be aware of what would help my business most and directly ask for it. As long as I am prepared to give in return then this is where collaboration starts to help women in business to work together and support each other.

Don't be embarrassed about asking for what your business needs. In my group we have 'wing woman Wednesday' every week where the group can ask for what they need. Please share this post for me, please can I have some engagement here, please can I have some feedback or whatever. We genuinely have people in the group who tell me that even with the opportunity right there they don't know what to ask for. Wait, what? You really don't have a social media post you'd like some shares or interaction on at the very least. I mean just pick your most recent one if you really aren't sure. Whatever you do, don't let the opportunity pass you by.

The group delivered and we had one our most successful nights for the business in open class bookings. I asked for and got what I wanted. It was more than that though. I realised that by talking honestly about my experiences for good and bad, I was opening up the floor for other women in business to do the same. My inbox was bursting with stories of women leaving jobs that weren't working for them following motherhood. Leaving promising careers because the world of work had become a battleground instead of stepping stones to the lives that they wanted.

The sheer fact that women face so many barriers to the world of work and business infuriates me but what really tugged at my heart strings is that these women felt that they were alone in their story. That there must have been something wrong with them. If only they hadn't got pregnant when they did, if only they'd worked harder or changed this and that then the inevitable barriers that they had seen wouldn't have cropped up. Yet, of course they would. These women weren't to blame but the wall of silence around why women had suddenly jumped into their business amidst the hard-balancing act of returning to work had left them feeling alone. This just made me even more determined to keep supporting my group. That fire had been lit and there was no going back so I just leaned into it. When you know what lights your fire, move towards it. I'd had a hard fight to start to carve out the life that I wanted and I wasn't about to stop now. I felt like I had more to share, more to say and more to give so I went and got a coaching qualification.

In a way these skills were well aligned with all the soft skills I had developed during my career but I felt that it was important to cement them into something more concrete. I started to think of this idea of mums feeling lost in a labyrinth of motherhood which we now called the Mamarinth! Like Alice in Wonderland tumbling and twisting, women were finding themselves falling into this unknown world without a map. As they say, kids don't come with a manual and nor does motherhood. I created an online community in a Facebook group called 'Lost in the Mamarinth' where we can talk about why we feel lost in the mamarinth this week or how we've unreasonably managed to upset our children by doing something hideous like trying to give them the spaghetti and meatballs they asked for with a pasta sauce. You know, like how spaghetti and meatballs is made. The horror!

CARVING OUT MOMENTS OF CALM

Interestingly, this idea of carving out what you want has become a cornerstone of the group. The word self-care gets banded around when talking about how to cope with some of the common challenges and overwhelm of motherhood but in reality, for a busy business owner and mum of a young child, sometimes the idea of fitting in a yoga class, massage and bubble bath can just feel like more things I'll be failing to do. Women need ways to lift themselves up, not more to beat themselves with. Does that mean that a bubble bath or a yoga class are unrealistic? No, of course not. Are there some weeks where business is busy, the school have declared it purple panda appreciation week and I also agreed to help a friend with something important and it is therefore just not going to happen if I also decide that self-care needs to take hours and hours. Bingo!

In the Lost in the Mamarinth Facebook group we talk about carving out little moments or little pockets of calm. This could be a 10-minute meditation, a 10-minute yoga sequence, a nice coffee on a park bench by yourself, a short walk in the sunshine or whatever makes you feel good. Its short, its sweet, it's totally achievable and it makes the world of difference to women who are busy, stressed and find the idea of 'self-care' in the traditional sense a bit daunting. There are also women in the group who find the idea of carving out even 10 minutes to truly relax and do something for themselves too much. How crazy is that! 10 minutes! I absolutely get it though.

The school run has condensed by working day and being able to achieve the lifestyle I want where I am predominately the person collecting my daughter from school comes at the price of needing to be incredibly productive with the time that I have. I'll be the first to point out that where there are unsupportive partners who are not doing their fair share of family life then this is unacceptable but not all women in the group have another adult in their home. Some of them have no family support at all. Would of, should of, could of highlights issues but we want more than that. We want to offer easy, practical ways to improve life. Women need to start to open up and build up their resources to crawl back through the layers of the Mamarinth because some are pulled deep into the centre. Some of these moments are scheduled but many are spontaneous, cheap and feel good.

CARVING OUT WHAT YOU WANT

As I was carving out the life that I wanted, I was faced with an uncomfortable reality. I didn't really know what I wanted. I hadn't ever particularly taken the time to think about what I wanted. I had followed a path laid out for me where ponds led to rivers and rivers led to oceans, with me floating through life and my career. What was there to think about? A job came up that I could do and offered me a little more money and boom, there I was. There was no real depth or creativity to how I was thinking about my life. Then when I found the endless possibilities and freedom of self-employment it felt like learning to walk again. My mind couldn't cope with everything I could do. I don't consider myself particularly spiritual or 'Woo' but a friend got me into the idea of manifesting and in typical me fashion, I went about it the most practical way that I possibly could.

When it was described as manifesting I was convinced that it couldn't possibly work but when I thought about it, what it really was were ways to open up my mind to what I wanted and setting achievable goals. Its far easier to achieve what you want if you are actually bringing into your awareness what that is. Yet it's a common stumbling block for many women who have built their lives around others or dedicated themselves to motherhood to the point that they have almost faded away themselves. I bought myself a little purple notebook from the supermarket and kept it by my bed with a pen. Each night I would brain dump whatever came into my head about what I wanted. It didn't matter how small, how big or how ridiculous, I wrote it down!

When I talk to Mamarinth mums about manifesting I always remind them that writing something down on paper isn't signing your life away. Just write it down. Who cares how silly it is. When I start to notice themes and things reoccurring then I know that these are things that I really want and where to focus my attention. Manifesting simply means to make real and I set about making real some of the goals that I had written down.

So, what I did I manifest? A business award, a home office come Zoom studio for online first aid classes, extra sources of income, regular experiences and a whole lot more. These were the things that were important to me and before I knew it I was making tangible things happen that sent ripples throughout my life. Manifesting doesn't always mean dreaming that a new house or car will fall into your lap. For me, it was about real and easy changes to get to what I really wanted. When I realised how important having space to work at home was, it didn't take me long to declutter the spare room and make it happen. My home office come Zoom studio was born in less than a week.

CARVING OUT THE INCOME THAT YOU WANT

Let's talk money. It may be true that money isn't everything but I wasn't going to achieve the lifestyle I wanted or some of the goals that I had without a drastic overhaul of my income. In the heart of the public sector, the wage I was taking home wasn't getting me very far for all of my hard work; especially with childcare costs. There is something about aspirational women that can sometimes make other women uncomfortable. Rev that bulldozer! I'm not about to let anyone's expectations of me or their discomfort hold me back. I don't see why I should be ashamed of being able to pay my bills with the income from my business; surely that's the point of self-employment? Yet there almost seems to be an expectation that self-employment should come with struggle. No thanks. Hard work, dedication, passionate and good decision making? Absolutely, but struggle? No. Some people almost seem happier struggling in their business than when they are succeeding but a struggle is only a failure if you don't learn from it.

Difficult things and bumps in the road crop up in business as they do in life. Learn from them. Move towards the things that are bringing you success and carve out the path and income that you want. I don't mind people seeing my aspiration. I want clients to know that the business is doing well. I hate in when I see business pages full of moans and groans about customers. Some businesses seem happy to demand respect without giving the same to the customers who they want to part with their hard-earned money. If you have boundaries and attract the right customers to you whilst moving your business forward in the direction that you want it to go then this really isn't an issue. No one is buying from a business that is constantly moaning at them through their phone because someone missed a bill, broke the loo or got a bit loud mouthed. If you have a handful of customers that misbehave then deal with them.

Don't tell off your entire following and decide that your business only deals with people who disrespect you or that is exactly what you will attract. Its controversial but when I see these posts it is clear that someone is just farming sympathy to make themselves feel big because their mum or best friend comments about how awful it is. Dealing with issues isn't for social media. I make sure I always get paid rather than moaning about it. I have had people try to tell me that because I'm aspirational and push for business growth that I 'must be in it for the wrong reasons' or should wait until my four-year-old is older because 'maybe it's just not your time right now'. What? Mothers of young children are exactly the group who need to get serious about their income and their finances because I have a little person who is relying on me and watching how I live my life. I want to show her that she can follow her dreams and aspirations and be a mother if she chooses. Their discomfort doesn't need to become mine. I'm totally fine with my business goals and aims. A business that makes money, is stable, supports other women, supports families and does good is a business worth my time.

Don't be ashamed of making money, of making good decisions and of setting goals for yourself. Having money goals has not only helped keep me focus and lazy manifest my way to what I want, it helps me get real about my finances and celebrate my wins along the way. If I know that I need X amount to get the lifestyle that I want then it's a hell of a lot easier for me to work out what my businesses need to do and what I need to do to make that happen.

YOUR PATH AWAITS IF YOU HAVE THE COURAGE TO CARVE IT OUT FOR YOURSELF......

Printed in Great Britain
by Amazon